Dancing With Danger

Dancing With Danger

by Clive E. Neil

END TIME WAVE
PUBLICATIONS

Whitehouse Station, New Jersey

Dancing With Danger

ISBN 1-889389-11-0

Table of Contents

ACKNOWLEDGMENTS

I must convey my indebtedness to the officers, members, and friends of Bedford Central Presbyterian Church. Their love for Christ has taken their collective will to turn obstacles into opportunities of a new level.

To my partner and friend Faye whose constant challenge and support keep me motivated. To my children, Aisha and Darius, for their questions about how I cope with all the obstacles in my life. To Cecilia Channell-Cherry and Agnes Alexander for their typing and editorial assistance, and finally to my parents who—— despite tremendous difficulties—— have a deep joy which has laid a foundation for me to emulate.

FOREWORD

Welcome to the real world, especially for Christians. This may be an unfamiliar environment for contemporary Christians. Unfortunately, the most popular versions of Christianity today seem to promote the notion that Christians are not real people who live in the real world with all of its inherent problems and challenges. We are often lead to believe that if we have accepted Christ as our personal Savior and Lord, we have been raptured out of the real world of human faults and frailties to some fantasy land of "once upon a time" and they lived perfect and happy ever after. And then for those Christians who at their conversion didn't quite get raptured out of the real world, they were told that their Christian faith carried with it a formula for health, wealth and success. So these Christians go around "teaching the Word" of this very attractive but very unreal brand of Christianity as normative for all.

Of course, those of us who are their brothers and sisters who are wise enough, spiritually mature enough and intellectually honest enough to accept the faults and frailties of our own humanity, we know the rest of the story. We know that so many of these "babes in Christ" are living in a fantasy land, totally out of touch with reality and thereby ineffective witnesses for Christ. They are often at the breaking point, frantically searching for answers in quick fixes from the faith, proof-texting from the Scriptures and misinterpreting the Word, seeking simplistic spiritual solutions and various other substitutes for authentic discipleship. The tragedy is that they are living the Christian life in an atmosphere of "quiet desperation."

In this book Dr. Clive E. Neil endeavors to show us how to work out of a new perspective on the obstacles which Christians encounter. He suggests that one can find strength and insights from the Scriptures that can feed the inner person to effectively deal with challenges. The book lays out some of the profound insights in the Christian gospel message that will enable believers to handle the adversities of life. Dr. Neil is a Pastor and a Scholar, who, with his passion and perceptive insights speaks healing and hope amidst the complexities of human life.

Thank God, Here's hope. Dr. Neil combines his calling as a Christian minister and psychotherapist to give the best of both worlds. He diagnoses our diseases and prescribes good medicine to cure the plagues of practical Christian living.

I thank God for courageous persons, like Dr. Neil who speak to the pain and promise in our relationship with God. With a therapeutic savvy, keen wisdom, liberating exegesis, and divine anointing, he ministers to all of us. The shared gifts of his mind, person and spirit will challenge you, inspire you, teach you, convict you and empower you. He speaks the truth and the truth will set us free.

This book is a necessary tool in the libraries of those who desire change. Here's help, healing and wholeness.

Dr. Arlee Griffin, Senior Pastor
Berean Baptist Church
Brooklyn, NY

INTRODUCTION

The gifted 19th century violinist Niccolo Paganini was standing before a packed house playing through a difficult piece of music. A full orchestra surrounded him with magnificent support. Suddenly one string on his guitar snapped and hung gloriously down from his instrument. Beads of perspiration popped out on his forehead. He frowned but continued to play, improvising beautifully. To the conductor's surprise, a second string broke, and shortly thereafter, a third. Now there were three limp strings dangling from Paganini's violin as the master performer completed the difficult composition on the remaining string. The audience jumped to its feet and, in splendid fashion, filled the hall with shouts and screams of "Bravo! Bravo!" As the applause died down, the violinist asked the people to return to their seats. Even though they knew there was no way they could expect an encore, they quietly sank back into their seats. He held the violin high for everyone to see. With the desire so strong for an encore and with a twinkle in his eye, he played the final piece on one string as the audience shook their heads in silent amazement. What an attitude in a moment of difficulty!

Words can never adequately convey the incredible impact of our perspective towards life. The longer I live, the more convinced I become that life is 10% what happens to us and 90% how we respond to it. How else can anyone explain the unbelievable feat of hurting athletes? I believe the single most significant decision I can make on a daily basis is my choice of attitude. It is more important than my past, my education, my bankroll, my successes or failures, fame or pain, or what people think or say about me, and even more important than my circumstances or my position; for my responding attitude towards the obstacles in my life will keep me going or cripple my progress. It alone fuels my fire or assaults my hope. When my perspective is right, there is no dream too extreme, nor challenge too great for me. Yet, we must admit that we spend more of our time concentrating and fretting over the strings that snap and dangle— the things that cannot be changed— than we do giving attention to the one string that remains by our choice of attitude. Stop and think about some of the things that suck up our attention and energy, all of them inescapable. For example— the weather; people's actions and reactions; delays at airports, demands of a workload; or the cost of groceries. The greatest waste of energy in our ecologically minded world of the 1990's is not electricity or natural gas or any other "product," but rather it is the energy we waste fighting the inevitable. And to make matters worse, we are the ones who become twisted, negative, and tight-fisted fighters.

Paul, in Philippians 2:5-8, suggests that it was a special kind of attitude that brought the Savior down to us. Jesus deliberately chose to come among us because He realized and valued our need. Christ placed a higher significance on our need than on His own comfort and prestigious position. In humility, Jesus set aside the glory of heaven and came to be among us. Jesus refused to let His position keep us at arms length.

It is virtually impossible to complete a day without being confronted by some obstacles. This makes it easy to pick up the habit of negative thinking because so much around us prompts us to be irritable. Let's not kid ourselves, life is not a bed of roses. One way of beginning to change our perspective is by accepting the attitudes of joy. According to Paul in Philippians, joy is not fickle, needing a lot of "things" to keep us smiling. Joy is deep and consistent. It is that oil which reduces the friction of life. Our minds can be kept free of anxiety as we dump the load of our cares on the Lord in prayer. By getting rid of the stuff that drags us down, we ✗ create space for joy to take its place.

Think of it like this: circumstances occur that could easily crush us. They may originate on the job, at home, or even during the weekend when we are relaxing— but unexpectedly, they come. Immediately we have a chance to make an attitude choice. We can either hand the circumstances to God and ask God to take control, or we can roll up our mental sleeves and slug it out. Joy awaits our decision. If we do as Philippians 4:6-7 suggests, then peace replaces panic and joy moves into action. Joy is always ready but it is not pushy. Let's not kid ourselves either when we deliberately choose not to stay positive and we deny joy a place in our lives, we will usually gravitate in one of two directions— or sometimes both— the direction to blame or self pity.

I have been greatly encouraged and strengthened by the story of Joni Erickson who in 1967 experienced a broken neck. She lost all feeling from her shoulder down. Despite numerous operations, her reality became broken romance, the death of dreams, no more swimming, horseback riding, skating, running, dancing, not even a stroll ever again. All those strings now dangled from her life. Yet, whenever she ministered there was a radiance, a remarkable joy from this rare woman who had chosen not to quit.

This book is about those who have faced obstacles but desire to turn them into opportunities for God. These reflections are written with those persons in mind who continue to struggle with problems that blind them to the possibility of a new perspective. Come and explore these reflections of relevant issues of today, and then discover new ways of turning these obstacles into possibilities, using God's power.

CHAPTER ONE

PUTTING WISDOM TO WORK

I would like to attempt to address some practical problems of the Christian life. This book is not designed to be enjoyable, and I suspect it will not be the kind of book that will bring delight, but I do hope it will be enlightening and encouraging for us to deal with some of the issues that we as people face. Preachers are notorious for answering questions that no one is asking and leaving out the answers to the questions which everyone wants. So, in this book I want to zero in on those issues that concern all of us.

Let me set the stage for this book with these four clarifying statements. It is incorrect to think that because we are Christians all of our problems are solved. I think we do disservice to others when we bait unbelievers by telling them to come to Christ and all of their problems will be solved. The Bible never says that, but it does promise that we would be new creatures and assures us that we will have a destiny that is secure. It does not tell us that we would have no problems once we become Christians. The Bible does not tell us that Christians will be immune from the problems of life.

⅄ The second fact is that it is incorrect to say that all problems are discussed in the Bible. They are not. It is unwise for us to get into areas where the Scriptures do not speak. That is why I will base everything on Scriptures, and wherever I get off I may be on shaky soil. The Bible does not answer all of the problems we face.

Thirdly, it is incorrect to believe that because one has a problem that the person is unspiritual. It is dangerous that this attitude is conveyed in so many places today. Having a problem simply proves that we are human. If there is anyone who does not have a single problem, it would be interesting to see what that person is like. We are not unspiritual because we are wrestling with something. Some of the most spiritual people wrestle with some of the deepest problems of life. For example, look at Job. He faced the problem of suffering, and he did not have an answer or understanding as to why— and his counselors could not help him either.

The fourth fact is that it is incorrect to assume that because we have been exposed to Bible teachings we automatically know how to solve problems. Bible instruction alone will not solve problems. It is a map, however, just looking at a map will not result in our reaching the desired destinations. We just have the map to tell us how to get there, but getting there means we have to make the necessary effort to go through the experience, take the time for travel. In Hebrews 5:11-14 the writer is talking about maturity and the lack of it. Speaking of Melchizedek he said, "The people have heard the word but have not applied it. They have listened but have become hard of listening, dull of hearing." What is the sign of maturity? It is practicing that which one hears because as we practice we become mature. It is one thing to grow old in the Lord; it is another thing to grow up in the Lord.

Many people travel from church to church, from one Bible conference to another, filling notebook after notebook with notes— yet still they are the crankiest, most immature people you can be around. Why? Because of a lack of practice of the things which they have heard. God wants us to put to the test the promises He gave us. What we do is speak so loudly that we, ourselves, cannot hear the words. The sign of a mature person is one who is practicing on a regular, consistent basis what one hears. Maturity is a process which we constantly absorb by spiritual osmosis.

When irritation comes, we apply the Scriptures which deal with irritation. When temptation comes, we apply the principles of Scripture that help us feast victoriously over temptation. When the sins of the flesh arise, we apply principles that we have been instructed to use for this area. Consequently, in the experience of such application we become wise and mature.

It would be erroneous for a person to go to a physician and say I have a growth and for the physician to say the growth will be removed. That individual would have to be operated on because just mere exposure of the problem will not make us mature nor will it resolve the issue.

The only thing our leaders can do is expose us to the Bible. It has no magic potion for us to rub on ourselves or slip under the pillow, and suddenly all of God's truths are known. There is no instant maturity known on this earth. It is through the hard core, gutsy job of applying what we hear.

Now in the Book of Proverbs, our Lord tells us about a famous character named Solomon. He was raised in a rich heritage. He was the son of David with vast experience, he was a king of Israel. Solomon was not perfect, but God lead Solomon to write the Proverbs which are contained in the Bible, and they come from the man who was both the wealthiest and wisest who ever lived. He had more wisdom than any person, but he was still a person with unsolved problems.

The question one must ask is why will I benefit from a study of Proverbs? Therefore, we must observe four specific statements concerning Proverbs.

1. To know wisdom and instruction. This is the first benefit of studying Proverbs— we can gain wisdom. What is wisdom? There are many definitions we have heard. But wisdom is the application of truth to experience, looking at life from God's point of view; seeing life as God sees it. As we see life as God sees it, we are able to see through it, not just look at it. Wisdom is understanding the life which God has given us to live and being able to deal with it victoriously.

Someone has said, "Psalms is a book that teaches us to get along with God. Proverbs is a book that teaches us how to get along with people. Psalms is a vertical book, Proverbs is a horizontal book. Psalms brings us into the heavenly, Proverbs sets our feet in the grassroots of human life." If we want to be wise, then we need to become students of Proverbs. There are 31 chapters, and they fit neatly into 31 days of the month. If we should read through the Book of Proverbs three times and apply it, we will learn wisdom.

2. We will learn to discern the things of understanding. So, in this book there are treasures of understanding. What is understanding? While wisdom is looking at life from

God's view point, understanding is responding to life from God's view point. Wisdom is an act; understanding is a reaction. Wisdom is that which we assert; understanding is the way we respond to those things that life brings our way.

3.   This passage says that we will receive instruction in wise behavior. A spiritually-minded young person wants to be wise. It is a promise that if we become prudent students of Proverbs, we will be wise with discretion. There is not another book that can make that kind of promise. There are 186 kinds of people mentioned in the Book of Proverbs, and the person who came out on top is the wisest person, the one who knows how to handle life from God's point of view. Notice in verse 20, that Solomon suggests that wisdom is available. God has not taken the gift of wisdom and tucked it away in heaven for it to await us there to be opened. Rather, Solomon says that wisdom is available right now, and it is crying for us to let it in.

4.   Verse 24 suggests that wisdom can be spurned. Our problem is not exposure, but our problem is the lack of experience entering into that which we are exposed. Wisdom says we can neglect her. Wisdom is available. The teaching of God's Word provides us with wisdom. So, if we want to gain wisdom we must begin in the Word of God.

We cannot begin to gain wisdom with experience as being the sole basis for our attainment of it. Our world is looking for experience. We have people who will stand in long lines to get an experience. People will travel the world to find a pleasing experience, and yet in the final analysis, they are still empty. Wisdom, as it is found in the pages of

God's Word, is available— but it can be spurned. That is the author's concern. It therefore follows that if we spurn wisdom, it will bear bitter fruit. What happens when we turn away the wisdom of God? What happens when we hear the truth of God and we reject it? According to verse 26, wisdom is not provided by God in a panic package. God doesn't suddenly give wisdom after we constantly reject it. Week after week and month after month, when the very bars of our lives are abruptly shaken, God will not suddenly give us wisdom. It comes over a process of time and so wisdom will not rush to our help after being rejected constantly.

Individuals come to us for counseling after they have been exposed to truth after many years. However, they did not accept the truth which they were exposed to and now suddenly they want help. It is virtually impossible to unknot those major problems of their lives. Wisdom doesn't suddenly come, but it comes over a process of time. My desire is that we learn how to be spiritually self-sustaining and glean from God's Word the substance we need to live.

Wisdom says if we keep turning her away, she will laugh at our calamity. It is always amazing that when people seek counseling it is because they have come at the end of their ropes or tolerance level. They only come after numerous times of ignoring God's truth and wanting suddenly a solution. Unfortunately for many, wisdom is not like that, and because we ignore wisdom we suffer, and the suffering is a logical process of the law of diminishing return. What I hope to build in our thinking is the importance of regular obedience to God's Word — not to live perfectly, but to live wisely. When wrong comes do not let it stack up, rather deal with it instantly. If we refuse to do this, then we will eat the fruit of our labor.

Think about Samson who, after twenty years of judging Israel, ran into a harlot and then went back to Delilah, which resulted in his eyes being plucked from his skull, hair shaved and turned into a miserable clown. Samson illustrates that sin blinds, grinds, and binds. When we let sin continue in our lives, it never solves itself— it only brings another sin. The wise person is one who deals with it.

Verse 22 refers to three other kinds of people. The simple, the scorners, and the fool. A simple person in the Hebrew suggests a wide open door. What is a simple person? One who is easily lead and misled, lacking discernment. A simple person is the one whom the cults of our day feed upon because he/she lacks insight and is, therefore, open to any wind or current that may blow their way. Paul mentions it in Ephesians 4 when he says, "Let us not be children." Children are simple, but that is part of being childlike— they can be easily led. However, when one grows spiritually he/she is no longer simple and wide open to any counsel without discernment. What does Proverbs says about this person? That if we are easily seduced, we are simple. The simple one forgets that down at the end of the road there are consequences. Solomon says if we are simple then we lack understanding. Simple people seem to believe everything. They just give themselves to whatever they hear. The simple hide themselves and continue to make the same mistakes over and over again, suffering the same consequences for his/her foolish acts. God's desire for us is that we learn from our mistakes and refuse to do them over again.

In Proverbs 4:1, we are told of the prudent person, who has the ability to strip away and see what is really there. Our parents' advice might be difficult to take, for they have learned to see through people and they share with us their wisdom. Wise is the person who learns to respect the advice of parents. God rewards us for obedience. Our parents want us to be prudent, to be able to strip away the mask.

The scorners are the second kind of persons that Solomon spoke about. The scorners have a nature to turn aside, to reject, to mock, to refuse, or to be disgusted. The scorners have one rebuttal after another, along with a tendency to fill their mouths with a fist. That will not do the job. Proverbs 9:7 says, "do not correct a scorner, for he/she will hate you; only correct a wise person, for they will love you."

Let me now analyze the person whom the Scripture calls a fool. We don't use this word much these days, but let me suspend subtle diplomacy so that we may hear how God tells it straight. It occurred to me recently that I like straight talk from three people in particular— from my accountant, my car mechanic, and my doctor. In the same way, God talks straight out about this person called a fool; both Psalms and Proverbs say a lot about the fool, digging deeply to show us the person on the inside. Psalm 14:1 gives an exact definition. It removes the notion of a fool being a mischievous person or a practical joker. That is not the fool painted on the pages of Scripture. When the fool is mentioned in Scripture, he/she is one who says down in his/her heart that there really is no God to worry about. There is no divine accountability. "What is all this business about God's high and holy standard, God's great character?" the fool says. The fool sincerely doubts God's existence and believes that he/she is free to live as one's own god. Therefore, it is no surprise that the fool lives a life of corruption as one who says there is no God and invariably lives lower than the standard of God. The fool speaks that language which denies God in the heart because there is a certain bent on self-will. Proverbs 4:8 mentions this bent of will. This verse suggests that you can count on a fool to lie to you because they are deceivers of people. When it comes to doing wrong, the fool makes light of it, and sometimes it comes out in profanity or dirty jokes. They possess a snaring cynicism of sin. They speak of wickedness like it is a sport. The practice of wickedness brings the fool personal pleasure rather than grieving. The fool finds delight in wickedness as a sport to do wrong. This does not mean the fool is intellectually defective. They can be very bright with impressive degrees. Folly has nothing to do with IQ but has everything to do with stupidity. To quote Shakespeare in MacBeth, "a tale told to an idiot is full of sound and fury, and significantly nothing else." This is not just characterized by deception, mockery, and the sport of wickedness but the entire person rages against the Lord.

There are three groups of people who will not gain God's wisdom because they will not hear God's reproof, and they are the simple, scorners, and the fool. The question then becomes what is so great about this wisdom? Why is it worth coming home to? Why shouldn't I run wild to follow the urges of my emotion? Why not let it all hang out? What is the big deal with wisdom? First, let's listen to Solomon from Ecclesiastes 7:11-14 and see that wisdom offers two major benefits: (1) wisdom preserves our lives from human pitfalls. Solomon gave us examples of such pitfalls. With an inheritance comes pride, so wisdom preserves us from that fault. Then there is the pitfall of affliction which leads to doubt and disillusion. With the anticipation of relief, vindication or reward comes the pitfall of resentment and bitterness. Wisdom preserves us from this as well. Solomon is absolutely correct that wisdom is protection. (2) Wisdom provides our lives with a divine perspective. We are first told to consider the Word of God and then told to develop the perspective we need. "Who is able to straighten what God has bent?" God is ultimately in control, and Solomon admonishes us with "in time of prosperity be happy and enjoy it." Divine perspective frees us to be truly happy. "But in time of adversity consider God who has made the one as well as the other." This divine perspective reminds us that God is just as caring in adversity as God is during time of prosperity. The Hebrew term "consider" suggests examining for the purpose of evaluation. In the hard times when the bottom drops out of our lives, when there are times of financial reversal or severe domestic or physical conflict, wisdom allows us to examine and evaluate with incredible objectivity. The good news is this— that such wisdom is ours to claim through an intimate relationship with God's own Son. Jesus Christ is the channel through which wisdom comes. In coming by faith to Christ, we are given open access to the wisdom of God. With the Son of God comes the wisdom of God.

CHAPTER TWO

THE TACTICS OF TEMPTATION

Mark Antony was known as the silver-throated orator of Rome. He was a brilliant statesman, magnificent in battle and courage. He was handsome. He had all the qualities of becoming a ruler of the world. However, he had in his life the very fateful and vulnerable fault of moral wickedness. So much so, that his personal tutor said to him: "Oh Marcus of Colossal, you are able to conquer the world but you are unable to resist temptation."

That indictment, I'm afraid, applies not only to Mark Antony— and not just to the people in the unsaved world —but also is applicable to us in the faith. We all face the reality of temptation. It is a real fact and some of us have not yet found an answer to how to overcome and resist temptation when it appears. This is exactly where we are. Therefore, I want to deal with several issues of temptation: (1) what temptation is; (2) why is it so successful; (3) what makes it work; (4) how can we handle it; (5) how can we learn what Mark Antony never learned.

The book of James is where we want to turn for most of this message. We understand that this book was written by James under the Spirit's inspiration, and that he wrote it to a group of people who were undergoing a number of difficult situations, among which included the fact that they were scattered abroad. We read that James was a bond servant writing to this scattered people, a condition which in and of itself imputes loneliness and temptation. These people were encountering all kinds of trials, and James wanted them to maintain their joy in the midst of difficulties.

From verse 1-12, he talks about trials. But when he gets to verse 13, the focus changes to something else called temptation. There is a difference between trials and temptation. Trials are ordeals or tests of our faith, and in trials there is not necessarily an evil connotation. Usually there is nothing immoral in experiencing a trial. A trial is a test, a hardship, an ordeal, but not usually evil or brought about by evil. For example, the trials of Job. He lost his health, family, and business, but there was nothing immoral about Job's experiences. It was a test, an ordeal. For a moment, reflect on Elijah under the Juniper tree. His life was threatened, and he pleaded with God to "Take my life. It is better that I die." There was nothing immoral about Elijah's experience. His issue of depression was an ordeal, a test. When John the Revelator was banished to the island of Patmos, there was nothing immoral involved. It was a test of his loneliness, having been removed from all that was familiar— presenting a trial. However, when we get to temptation there is a difference. As you can see in verse 13, the word used here is "tempted". Trial and temptation come from the same root word because in the mind of the writer, it was a different thing. The Webster Dictionary says temptation is the act of enticement to do wrong by promise of pleasure or gain which is supposedly good. As we mention temptation, we always imply that sensual aspect of it. Therefore, I would be willing to wager that if I took a poll and ask what is temptation, the vast majority of you would say that it is the sensual part of life, that which is lustful to the eye. That is just one aspect of it. We can be tempted to gossip, take something that it is not ours, hold a grudge, fight back, defend ourselves. So as we talk about it don't categorize it to relate to the sensual only.

Let's look at Galatians 5. Temptation should be counteracted by a particular act. It is called one of the fruits of the Spirit. In verse 5:23, we read that one way to counteract temptation is self-control. The word really means inner strength— the mastering of self. One of the things the Spirit promises to do for the child of God is to enable him or her to master one's self, our weaknesses or areas of need. That is the job of the Holy Spirit. Now, you probably state that "it is not something which I do, it is something God does." I'm just passively involved, and God is positively involved. Listen, self-control may come from the Spirit of God but we pave the way for it.

If we are passive and God is active, we just passively wait on God and He does it - and therefore we should not get involved with it. That sounds good but, practically speaking, it leaves a person with the wrong idea. That's virtually uninvolved in my life. Let me tell you, if we passively deal with temptation, it will conquer us everyday of our lives, even though the fruit of the Spirit is available.

Self-control comes from God but we pave the way for it. How do we know that II Peter 1:4 talks about the self-control? In that series of commands, God includes our responsibility to supply self-control. Galatians says it is the fruit of the Spirit— an ingredient from Heaven that God gives us when we come to know His Son. When the Spirit of God lives within us there is self-control, but Peter says supply it. We are to pave the way for it to take place. The ingredient is given to every child of God, but it is the responsibility of the child of God to make sure the way is open for self-control to take place.

James 1:13-15 talks about the solicitation to evil. There are four principles in response to temptation. Let's look at the following principles in these verses. The first principle is found in verse 13. Temptation is inevitable and unavoidable. "Let no one say when he is tempted that he is tempted by God." The author did not say if he is tempted, but he said when he is tempted. There is a difference between the two. It would be wonderful if we could live without temptation, but the simple fact is that we cannot. If we are trying to find some perfect place like an uninhabited island or secret area where there is no chance of temptation, don't move there because when you do, you will spoil it. When we go there we take our minds and our thoughts, which is the beginning of temptation. The point is we will never be in a place where there will not be any temptation. The monk who lives behind the wall wrestles with temptation as much as the business person who lives in the world today. The salesperson wrestles with it, just as the servants of the ministry.

Every one of us faces temptation because it is unavoidable and we cannot get away from it. I appreciate the fact that Scripture does not hide this truth. It is practical and doesn't make us feel guilty because we have temptations. There is nothing wrong in feeling temptation or having tempting things come before us. Therefore, notice that James says "let no one say they are tempted by God." Have you ever found yourself to say this? The classic case is Adam in the Garden of Eden. When he ate the fruit and was confronted by God, he said "the woman that You gave me, made me eat!" You can imagine that Adam went on to say "God you set me up! Here I was, enjoying the bounty and blessing of the Garden and here comes the female whom You brought into my life. She caused me to be tempted."

At times, we may think we are being tempted by God. There is something we cannot see in the English; there are two ways of describing agency in the New Testament, either directly or indirectly. This is indirect, called indirect personal agency. Let no one say when he is tempted that God is indirectly involved in my action. The point is God is not even indirectly involved in bring us into sin. We can be sure that God permits the events in our lives to take place, but when we yield to the temptation before us, God has nothing to do with that act. The action has sprung from the inner nature, the cesspool heart of us all. When we respond to sin in that temptation, God is not involved. Why not? How could it be? Let's look at the next two principles. (1) Temptation is never directed by God. He may permit it but never directs it. God does not direct us into sin. God cannot be tempted by evil, and God cannot tempt. Remember the words of John that, "God is light and in Him is no darkness at all." God cannot fellowship with nor tolerate sin. Therefore He cannot direct us into it. If we sin, it is our own choice because God is light. When the angels worshiped God in Isaiah 6, they rendered Him the praise of Holy, Holy, Holy is the Lord of Hosts— totally separated from sin. If God is separated from sin, then He cannot be involved in our sin and, therefore, He is not involved in our sin. This point brings us to the third principle.

In verse 14, temptation is an individual matter. "But each one is tempted when he/she is carried away in his/her own lust." It is important that each one own up to his/her actions. When we choose to yield to temptation, it is an individual matter. You cannot blame anyone else. Nothing is strong enough outside of us alone to cause us to sin. Sin takes place when we agree to that "thing" and get involved with it. But nothing outside of ourselves entices us. It takes an agreement such as when a metal object is drawn to a magnet. When that magnet appears and if there is no response, likewise the magnet may become stronger but that in itself is not sin. It is not until I— the individual involved— submit to the temptation and then sin takes place.

I have an attorney friend who works with Reserve Bank. His job involves trips to the Federal Reserve where there are numerous stacks of paper money for counting. I visited there one day and can attest that security there is extremely tight. There are cameras all around, and the employees are encased in bullet-proof glass everywhere, as they do nothing but count money. There were stacks of one hundred dollar bills, and I asked how can they stand being behind there. (This statement revealed something about my inner nature.) He said that everything is fine until they realize what they are doing! What did he mean? As long as he is counting slips of paper, he is fine. But when they suddenly realize "wow, this is a $100 bill!" — then they have problems. We can stack thousands of dollars in the air without any problem, but when we come to an internal realization that there is personal interest— there are potential problems!

This brings us to the fourth point. Temptation that leads to sin always follows the same process. Verse 14 begins the process and verse 15 carries it out. There are four steps for temptation as we see in verse 14-15. The outer bait is dropped: we can be hooked by temptation like a fish by a worm because we are hungry. When we fish, what do we do? We are dumb if we put a hook in the water without bait and expect to catch a fish. Why wouldn't you put a clothes pin or nail or belt? Why? because none of these appeal to a fish. We have to provide a bait that would attract a fish. Why a fish loves worms or shrimp we will not know, but fish will keep nipping until they get caught. Why? because you have chosen a bait that interests him. When that fish leaves its hiding place for the bait, he is caught just as we are when we leave our haven. We are protected, as long as we remain safe in our Lord and draw from Him our delight, zeal, for living. They can drop all kinds of bait and it wouldn't interest us. Yes, the temptation is there but if God's Word is stronger than anything out there, we can remain safe. When we leave from that hiding place and go looking for the bait we are gone - and we know it. So, we have a bait that is dropped along with an inner desire that is attracted to it.

Genesis 29 gives the classic way to handle temptation, in the story of Joseph and Potiphar's wife. Joseph was able to withstand the temptation because his heart for God was greater than his heart for anything on earth. He asked, "how can I sin this way against God?" Do not think that because you resisted it, it will end. The same tempting thoughts will come over and over because Satan doesn't quit, he only changes the bait. He will definitely find another way to get to us.

The next step: sin is conceived in the yielding. For a child to be born there has to be conception in the womb of the mother and the same is true for sin. For sin to be committed there is not only the magnet but the attachment. When sin is accomplished it brings forth death. When sin is achieved, it brings forth tragic circumstances. Temptation that leads to sin always follows these steps: (1) there is the bait; (2) there is an interest in the bait; (3) there is the reaching out for its yielding; (4) there are tragic results. Perhaps, I should say between the third and fourth there is a temporary period of pleasure. That is the lie that Satan uses as his ace trump. "You are going to receive pleasure or gain by doing this act."

I cannot, as a minister, leave you with the facts of temptation. How do we deal with what are some practical things we can do to pave the way for self-control to take over? So you ask, what can I do? As a human being with a nature that desires so much everyday of my life, how can I handle those things that are brought before me? Let's look at five things that can be helpful, useful, and practical. I must counteract temptation and not tolerate it. Place yourself in an area where you can go over them. Temptation must be counteracted! Romans 6:13— do not yield your members unto unrighteousness to sin, but yield yourself unto God. That's active— you cannot tolerate it. We play around with things that make us weak. We are weakened by certain kinds of music, we play into the hands of Satan. If we are weakened by a certain kind of film, then that film builds within us desire. We are not counteracting but we are tolerating it, or fertilizing it. Stay away from the news stands that destroy the mind. We are fools if we know that these things weaken us and we tolerate it. By constantly bringing this in front of our eyes, we play into the devil. I must use certain techniques with certain temptations. Do not play with sin or hang around it. Job 31:1, says we must make a covenant with our eyes. I have to make a covenant with my eyes— how then can I gaze at a virgin? The eye is that tempting part of life. Proverbs 4:25 says look straight ahead not to the right or left. It isn't the first glance but it is the second stare that leads one into sin.

To those of you who want to be rich and you are tempted in that regard, God says to be generous. If your temptation is to gossip, God says to avoid it. Say nothing so that you may pray more intelligently. If necessary, tell God instead about the person if you cannot trace the source of it. You must use certain techniques with certain temptations. For me, I must remind myself that it's the final pain which will soon erase the temporary pleasure that I'm passing up. That's what Moses did when he walked with God rather than getting caught up in Israel's lifestyle. In Hebrews 11:24-25, by faith Moses when he was grown up refused to be called the son of Pharaoh's daughter, choosing to endure ill treatment with the people of God rather than to enjoy the passing pleasures of sin. What an eloquent statement: the passing pleasures of sin - for this is so true. Sin is pleasurable, and as we turn off the internal warning signals and we turn on the desires. Dietrich Bonhoeffer the German theologian, who loved Jesus Christ, was hanged by the Nazi SS Black Guard on April 9, 1955, at age 39. He was a distinguished scholar and had won the acclaim of many reputable persons in Europe. His manuscript on temptation is one of the best articles I have seen on the subject. His dissertation was on our ability to turn off the warnings as sin winks at us, and I quote: "In our members there is a scrambling desire which is both sudden and fierce, which irresistible power desire seems to win over the flesh. Once the flesh burns, it makes no difference what kind of desire it is. Joy in God is extinguished in us as we seek all our joy in the creature. At that moment, God is unreal to us and loses all reality. Only desire for the creature is real. The only reality is the devil. Satan does not fill us with hatefulness of God but with forgetfulness of God. The power of clear distinction is taken from us. We must say it will not satisfy because in the end I will have to pay tremendous consequences and, therefore, I will not yield. God will honor such self-control.

I must control my thought life through the memorized Word when Satan launches his attacks full scale in subtle manner, often like erosion but it is effective. I must battle it on a daily basis. This is not mystical or unreachable. Saying no is something all of us who belong to Christ can do. As we put Christ at the center of our lives, we are given the inner strength to say no. The Lord will give us the power to say no."

In a quiet village south of Pittsburgh, a shiny, new red building was built to house the fire and police departments, and the people loved it. In a few months the building showed some obvious cracks, windows were closed, and the doors stayed ajar. The floor began to buckle and the sidewalk finally cracked. Within one year, the building was condemned. An expensive attack against Jesus in Matthew 4:1-11, and our Lord withstood temptation by using the Scripture. He said on three occasions, "It is written..." The Psalmist asked "how can a young person keep his/her way pure? By keeping it according to Thy word; Thy word have I hid in my heart that I might not sin against thee." (Psalm 119:11) When the Word of God is stored up in our minds, it stands ready to strike and no one can stand against the truth. Galatians 6 says "be not deceived because that which a person sowed they shall also reap." God's Book will keep us faithful. I must do battle on a daily basis to protect my temple. Temptation comes on from all angles and with different levels of intensity or subtlety. It can tear us down over time or overnight. An investigation was made and it was discovered that deep below the surface, the structure of the red building was built near some mining work. This building was destroyed because there was a flaw deep down underneath the surface. If we play with temptation, linger near the bait, over and over and over again, then down in the essence of our being— as with the building— permanent damage will occur that we cannot imagine. Let's come to terms with this now, or later on we will regret it.

CHAPTER THREE

BEWARE OF BITTERNESS

All of us have felt the sting of being wrongly accused or unfairly treated. And for some of us, those barbed memories have caused a swelling of bitterness. Many of our hearts are swollen with the poison of years-old resentment because we have refused to let Christ pull the thorns. We are like little children who cry about their pain to anyone who will listen but will not allow anyone to touch the sore. We have chosen to respond horizontally to injustice, rather than vertically; our focus is strictly on ourselves and the wrong done against us.

We do have another option, however. We can shift our focus to the vertical and choose to set our eyes on God, instead of on the wrongdoing. For most of us, though, our first reaction is that "this cannot be done; that sounds nice on paper, but out in the trenches of hurt feelings and ruptured relationships, it is impossible to carry out. However, there is someone who had done this. His name was Joseph, and his story is familiar to most of us. Let's look at Joseph again, not in the context of childhood in Sunday School classes, but in the real world of ill-treatment and tough choices.

Proverbs 2 says, "Children, if you will receive My Word and hide My commandment with you, so that you incline your ear to wisdom and incline your heart to understanding, if you cry after knowledge and lift up your heart for understanding, then will you understand the fear of the Lord and knowledge of God." We have to dig for the Lord's wisdom as we do for hidden treasures. How do we handle the problem of bitterness or resentment? I will discuss these two concerns as being in the same family. There are two different responses we can have to wrong doing when it comes into our lives. Many of us have experienced the reality of having been done wrong by someone when we have done right. That is a hard situation to handle, for it is hard enough to handle when we do wrong and to be under the gun or be judged for our actions. However, when we do right and suffer unjustly, it is extremely difficult to respond in a positive way.

Our response to injustice determines whether we become bitter or become more mature. Let's take the first possibility. It is what I call the problem of horizontal focus. If we are done wrong by someone, especially by a close friend or family member, and we have to the best of our understanding been doing right, then we have a decision to make. We can respond to wrong doing horizontally or vertically. Let's say we take it as a personal offense and determine in our minds to look at it strictly from the earthly point of view. Then, what we have put into process is a triangle experience. At least this wrong doing leads us to a peak that is a terrible experience to endure. I suppose most of us have experienced this mounting difficulty. Our first response is one of surprise that this person would have done us wrong. Our feeling is "I can't believe it," then our next response is hurt and worry. The hurt part says, "how could he/she do this to me?" The worry part says, "something else is happening that I don't know about," and it starts the tail spin of open hostility. Then the next response is doubt directed towards God: "Why did God let this happen to me? Why me? I have been faithful to God and suddenly this person has turned on me." This leads to bitterness: "I have had it!" People would say, "If this is the result of the Christian way of life, then I have had it." As a result, then comes the grudge with the determination to get even with that person: "I have done my best and this person has kicked me in the teeth or stabbed me in the back! I will get even! I will carefully wait for my time, then will open hostility take charge! Now is my time!" And all of this is in the process which results from the horizontal focus of bitterness.

I have sensed this in my own experience in the past as well as from people with whom I have dealt. Most of us have gone through these same feelings— those of bitterness because of wrong doing against us. There is a far better way to respond, which is what I call the vertical focus. In this case, wrong has been done against us, yet our response is correct. The most important issue is not the wrong, but God. The wise, mature, spirit-filled person responds with, "This is no accident. The Lord knows exactly what He is doing." This should be followed by, "God has allowed this for my good. I know that my response wasn't totally correct, but I know that behind the scenes God is working." We can reflect on Romans 8:28 which says, "For we know that all things work together for good." Therefore, we should continue with, "What is God trying to teach me since He is allowing this for my own good, using all experiences to show me what I must know. What should I learn at this time? How can I rebuild the relationship with this person?" In such humility, we are getting to the point where it really hurts because it is a rare Christian who is big enough to ask these questions— after someone has offended us. Frequently, we tend to believe that God teaches us a lot of things, but still resolve to have written that person off. Why? We have become tired of reaching out and sharing. We had become completely transparent with this person, and all we get in return is a knife in the back.

The person who is wise not only looks at a situation from God's point of view but says to himself or herself, "How can I build a relationship that is broken down? Have I completely forgiven this person? I can use the insight which I have gained from this experience. Since God is in the process of educating God's children— and since things do not happen by accident— and since God brings about things for our good— what are some of the things God wants to us to learn so that we can be on our way to maturity? Perhaps this all seems impossible because we feel that no one can really respond to wrong doing like that. Let's see if this perspective is right. Genesis 45 is part of the story of a great man. His name was Joseph. One particular characteristic of this person is that he is seen as his father's favorite son and, therefore, his brothers— out of jealousy— despised him. They turned against Joseph and, out of hatred, they sold him to a caravan on its way to Egypt. Joseph did not deserve that type of treatment. He was an innocent teenager who did not know how to handle that kind of favoritism. He was gifted beyond his years.

Joseph went to Egypt and became the house servant of Potiphar, who was an Egyptian in the monarchy. As a house servant, Potiphar's wife became attracted to him and made advances desiring to have him. Joseph did not yield, but she screamed and falsely accused him of taking advantage of her. Potiphar believed her and threw him in jail. Joseph did not deserve that sentence. While he was in jail, some of his companions formed friendships with him, and he helped them to know the future. They passed on Joseph's information to Potiphar of Egypt, but he told them before they got out of jail not to forget him. They were to make sure to tell the leaders the source of such vital information. Yet, they forgot him. He didn't deserve this neglect either. Two more years passed during this terrible jail ordeal in the dungeon, until finally he was taken from jail and became Prime Minister of Egypt. That, of course, was a real turn of events. In these few sentences, we have covered a lot of years in Joseph's life. His brothers, who sold him into slavery years before, were then at the time of his being Prime Minister— going through a famine back home. They had no idea that he was alive. They did not know that when they came to Egypt to find help and food, they would be standing in front of their long lost brother. That is where we find this family in Genesis 45. The important thing to remember is that this person Joseph had been done wrong on several occasions, but notice how he handled his situations vertically. Joseph never took his focus off God. He saw how God was at work in his life when they sold him into slavery. Joseph had the trip of a lifetime. God positioned him in such a way that he could actually be of help to his family. There was a tremendous lack of bitterness and resentment on Joseph's part. Instead, he was filled with love and compassion and interest in their welfare. It is interesting, that in our day and age there is developing an isolated, independent spirit among believers. I think it is significant that God frequently, in the majority of cases, dealt with families and not just individuals. In fact, God frequently brings to mind the situation that would appear to their families so that the entire family would experience it. Of whom did Joseph ask when he saw his brothers? His father. He wanted to know where his father was. How much do we care about our parents? What kind of relationship has been or is being developed if your parents are still alive? Joseph fell on his brother's neck and they wept. They experienced a oneness and unity, which they had never experienced before. Why? Because they had a brother who was big enough to say, "though you did me evil, God knew exactly what He was doing."

People who read this feel that this is unrealistic, suggesting that a person who does this has his/her head in the sand, and that person is not really being honest with his/herself. But there is a verse in this chapter that shows how realistic Joseph really had been. Verse 22 suggests that Joseph sent his brothers home with food and told them not to quarrel on their way home. This was such realism because he knew his brothers would get into an argument and never make it. He knew that they would cut each other off before they got back. So he told them not to quarrel on the way back.

A person who responds to life like this, in my opinion, is being extremely realistic. The difference is the person's point of focus. We live in a world that is horizontally oriented rather than vertically oriented. We are done wrong, and immediately we are told from the books we read and the counsel to whom we listen - to fight back, defend yourself, if we don't then no one else will. I admit that there are occasions when we must fight back— such as national defense, such as the invasion of personal or property rights. However, in more cases than not it is a matter of our personal rights being offended, and God has so many more things to teach us— that we may never learn because our response is horizontal. We are always poised to make sure no one is taking advantage of us. Joseph could have said, "I cannot wait to be Prime Minister so that I can take each one of my brothers by the throat and get back at them!" Instead, Joseph was the first to caution people about retaliation.

This position comes across clear in Chapter 50 of Genesis. Joseph had seen his father Jacob, who died briefly after their reacquaintance. Jacob saw his son Joseph and it was a thrilling family reunion. We need to notice verse 15. Joseph showed that his brothers couldn't believe their ears regarding his forgiveness. The same is true for people who turn against us or for those who dislike us, for in most cases they expect us to become enemies. They do not expect a relationship because it is one way of rejecting a person. These brothers heard with their ears and saw with their eyes Joseph when he said, "I forgive," but they didn't really believe that he could forgive enemies like they had been. His brothers were concerned that Joseph was holding a grudge to repay them for their mistreatment. The brothers needed constant reinforcement before they could accept Joseph's forgiveness.

We cannot fathom a person responding vertically. We are so experienced at being shot at that we cannot imagine when a person doesn't load up. Look sometimes at Proverbs 16:7 which says, "When a man's ways are pleasing to the Lord, He makes even his enemies to be at peace with him." If we are the first to take off the gloves, then others may follow. Of course, this is against the old nature, which tells us to keep the chips on our shoulders. Joseph did exactly what God wanted him to do and these fellows are saying, "we are your servants." Here lies the key nugget of the whole story. In Verse 20, "As for you brothers, you meant evil against me but God meant it for good." Why Joseph? In order to bring about this present result— to preserve the lives of many people. We can hear Joseph say, "I realized that if this experience had not occurred in my life, I would not have ended up in Egypt to become Prime Minister— ultimately being responsible for the store house of grain that would feed the generations to follow. Prophecy has been fulfilled because I was dumped in the pit."

When we are able to show forgiveness and compassion to someone who has done us wrong, then we are on our way. We should be a marvel in the human race. Joseph was realistic about his brothers' treatment but he just focused on

God, and God changed the course of history. What was the most important thing to Joseph? God. Verse 21 says, "Therefore, do not be afraid. I will prove for you and so he comforted them and spoke to their hearts." He spoke so that his spirit and their spirit experienced a marvelous unity. How many people can we really speak to in their heart? Can you do it with your mate, a friend? It may be that we cannot because we have never experienced it. To how many people can we say that we actually speak heart to heart? Let me share with you five lessons which I have gained from this story of counteracting bitterness. I asked God to make these things a reality in me. How do we counteract that old feeling which starts when we discover that someone has done us wrong?

First, we accept the reproof directly from God. This first step starts the ball rolling in the right direction. If we take the reproof as a personal offense, we are off target. If we take the reproof as directly from the hands of God, we are on our way to focusing correctly. The second thing I would suggest from the counsel of Joseph is to immediately seek God's help. Think offensively, not defensively. The reason I say this is that our tendency is to defend ourselves when we have been wronged. We tend to give four or five reasons to ourselves for why we don't deserve such an action. However, this begins a human tail spin that will never end. Since we are human, we will possibly be jolted or surprised when a close friend or relative turns against us. If we are not careful, days of depression will set in and we will be blue— for days, if not weeks and sometimes months. Someone stopped Billy Graham in England and remarked that if 70% of the persons in a mental institution could find forgiveness, they would be released. When we experience bitterness and if we soak it up long enough, we become sick people.

The third suggestion is to consider the other viewpoint. Do your best to put yourself in that other person's shoes and think about what they have said. We may be surprised because some of what they say may be justified completely to forgive them right there. This is where grudges are set. Grudges come from an unwillingness to look at an experience, a wrong doing, from the other person's point of view.

The fourth— stay positive and search for God's lesson. A person who is bitter frequently reveals his/her bitterness in negative reactions. They project a critical spirit, a frown, and long periods between smiles. I am not suggesting that life is one big bowl of jelly and that we will chuckle our way through it. However, a person who is bitter has a poor sense of humor or has lost their sense of humor because they feel they have been turned over to the torturous. One of the ways we can search for God's counsel is to have a close friend. "Iron sharpens iron, so the counsel of a person to a friend." Close, personal friends are known because they are confidantes. People who talk a lot are not our friends. They may be acquaintances but not close friends. Friendships are with people whom we can level and share our deepest conflicts and doubts, with confidence in knowing it will never go another step— and these kinds of persons are far and few in between. Deep friendship is based on confidentiality, security and absolute acceptance— which is rare. If you have found such a friendship, praise God! Perhaps what Joseph longed for most was a close friend.

Finally, discover ways of showing kindness to the other person. If we desire to see countenance fall and a shocked look, try showing kindness to a person who has done us wrong. I am not speaking here of hypocrisy, but rather a kindness that is absolutely genuine. We cannot reach this point until we have done the other steps which I have suggested. We are eating our hearts out in the Christian family in just these areas of bitterness and resentment. What I find stalking is that we are going to spend eternity with folks we cannot get along with for a few years in this lifetime. So we have our choice: We can each go on saying, "I don't deserve this and it is a total surprise and I am hurt! Why did God let it happen? It makes me so bitter. I have had it. I will get even. Now is my chance...!" or We can say, "What has happened is no accident. If the truth be known, I should have gotten worse treatment." True love doesn't take into account the wrong suffered. Maybe this forgiveness should start in our homes. There are situations that won't get better until we change. At the beginning of Psalms and throughout, we find David burdened, yet he closes with praise. God didn't change, David changed. Therefore, it is when we change that life becomes exciting.

CHAPTER FOUR

THE ANTICS OF ANGER

The great American statesman, Thomas Jefferson, worked out a way in which he handled his anger. It included a list of things which he believed that men and women must do to co-exist as adults. He wrote "When angry count to ten before you speak; when very angry count to 100." Mark Twain, about 75 years later, somewhat revised these words. He said, "when angry count to four; when very angry swear." Perhaps we have attempted to deal with our anger in one of these ways. Maybe you have counted to 4, 10, 100 or even swore, and it didn't seem to work.

There are some of us who say we have tried everything we can and we just can't seem to handle our anger. When we wrestle with a temper problem, we may smile on the outside but not on the inside, and I don't know of anything more frustrating to deal with than an anger problem. It has a way of disarming us, frustrating us, and taking away our testimony. Anger has a tremendous effect on our home life and our employment. It affects the people with whom we are closely associated, and they know that when the pressure is on, that's exactly what will happen. There will be a moment of intense anger.

In Ephesians Chapter 4 we are challenged by this very practical analysis of anger. What is anger? It is not easy to define. Webster doesn't help a lot. Psychologists provide a little something for us but not enough help. Therefore, I have woven several trends of thought together, and I came up with this definition: anger is an emotional reaction of hostility that brings personal displeasure to ourselves or someone else. People who studied the field say there are various phases of anger. We have experienced many of them. Anger can begin as a mild irritation which is nothing more than an irritation— a feeling of discomfort brought about by someone else or something. Then anger can turn from irritation to indignation; that is, a feeling that something must be answered back. There must be an avenger of that which is wrong or a punishment. Anger can go unexpressed as irritation can, but when irritation leads to indignation then anger becomes wrath. Wrath never goes unexpressed. People who are astute in the field tell us that wrath is a strong desire to avenge. Therefore, anger turns to fury - which suggests violence and even a loss of emotional control. Then the last phase of anger is rage. Rage is the most dangerous part of anger. This is a temporary loss of sanity, so that acts of violence are committed and the victims of anger scarcely realize what has taken place. That is why I say we can smile on the outside, but if we really wrestle with anger it's not funny. If we are given to those fits of fury or rage, then it's not a laughing matter at that point. We could probably all name homes that have been fractured or broken, where relationships are destroyed, and find at the heart of the problem one's anger.

We cannot solve the issue of anger in one sitting, but at least we can hear what God has to say about anger. We have read these verses often enough from Ephesians 4:26-27 to draw some observations. There are three issues that seem important. Do you realize God said to us, "Get mad! Be angry!" When was the last time we obeyed the Scripture and blew our stacks and just got mad?

The first observation of anger is that it is a God-given emotion. There is something inhumane about a person who never gets angry. God gives us emotions to show compassion, to show love. These emotions are God-given. The second observation is that anger is not necessarily sinful. There are times of anger that are not sinful, for not every expression of anger is wrong. We are told to be angry, but don't carry that anger to the point of it becoming sin. The third observation is anger must have safeguards. Paul named two of these safeguards. Someone may wonder if there is a proper time to be angry. Do you know that in the Old Testament the anger of God is mentioned 18 times? In the New Testament we have classic examples of Jesus' anger. When the money changers were in the temple He did not walk in and say, "listen friends, this is not good what you are doing." Rather, the Bible says that Jesus plotted together a whip and drove them out of the temple. This was an expression of real indignation. Jesus never spoke more angrily and forth rightly than He did to the hypocrite and the religious in Matthew 23— where in one case after another He said, "woe to you..." He called them snakes in the grass, vipers— and remember, that's Jesus speaking. So you see, there are times when anger is very appropriate but it must have its safeguards.

Paul gives two safeguards in Ephesians 4:26-27. The first safeguard is do not let the sun go down on our anger. Don't prolong anger into the night. In Paul's day, the setting of the sun was the close of the day. At the end of the day our anger/problem should be solved. This should be taken literally and practiced in our homes. When there are anger and disagreements during the day, they should be cleared up by the evening. When we lay down at night, we are to make sure these feelings of anger have been resolved. We are to make sure there is a clearing out of our conscience. We should not be deceived in thinking we can take care of it later on. Do not let sin come in by having our anger prolonged. There are some scars in our lives because we did not resolve the anger when it occurred. We went to sleep on it and it doesn't resolve itself. Instead, it stays and eats away like a bird at feeding time, until something else is formed and then comes the disease. The other safeguard is found in verse 27. Do not give the devil any opportunity. Do not allow our anger to be expressed in such a way that we are weakened and he reproduces his character through us. Remember that the devil is a counterfeit. Jesus loves to reproduce Christ's character through us. When we are under the control of the Holy Spirit, the character of Christ flows freely through us. Christ loves compassion, joy, and feelings of concern for others; but when we are given to the things of the devil and the old nature controls, then the devil reproduces the devil's lifestyle through us. That is Paul's point: don't let anger get a hold of us so we are weakened and other areas of sin are brought about. Also, remember that anger can so weaken us that the enemy reproduces his character in us.

When is anger justified? There are times when we can say from Scripture that it is right to be angry. In Exodus 32, the life of Moses is an adequate illustration of justified anger. In verse 19, Moses has been on Mount Sinai, receiving from the Lord the tablets of stone— known as the Ten Commandments. He had come down from the Mountain and looked at the people who had built an idol, and they were dancing in a lewd, profane fashion. Moses became angry and broke the tablets. Anger is justified when God's Word and will are consciously disobeyed by God's people. Anger is justified when sin is openly carried out and believers look on such behaviors placidly. In I Kings 11:1 is the very sad tale of the last part of Solomon's life. He had been blessed with riches and wisdom to perform more feats intellectually than any other man in Scripture. He had 1,000 women, and Solomon turned his heart away from his God. As verse 9 says "the Lord was angry because he turned away his heart from the Lord." God is angry when we openly and knowingly disobey God's Word. I am sorry that grace has been so twisted to convey that there are no standards any longer. For any of us to think there is not a quality of life expected now though we are under grace, that is a perversion and a lie. God still becomes intensely angry with us when we choose to openly disobey God's Word. There are other occasions when anger is justified as indicated in Isaiah, Chapter 5.

The second justifiable anger is when enemies move into realms outside their rights and jurisdiction. In Isaiah 5:20-23 we have enemies of the Lord moving in for territories outside of their rights, and the Lord rebuked them for it. "Woe to those who take away the rights of the ones who are in the rights." An example would be in I Samuel 11. Saul is the anointed king when an enemy came to invade the land, and the anger of Saul was greatly increased within him. His anger became intense because war had been declared against the land of God. The freedom of the people of Israel was being threatened. When an enemy decides to take the freedom of our land, we cannot sit back and accept that placidly, considering that it's just one of those problems in life. The Scriptures declare that when there are those who take away the rights of the ones who are in the right, even the Lord becomes angry.

A third area of justifiable anger is when parents are unfair to their children. In Ephesians 6:4, "Fathers, do not provoke your children to anger but bring them up in the discipline and instruction of the Lord." Fathers, do not deal with your children so that they are provoked to anger. It seems that fathers give in to impatience and give in to a lack of real understanding of the feelings of their little ones, or teens, or young adults. When we exacerbate our children unfairly, they respond in anger. We, as fathers, tend to get into a hurry and don't want to take time to listen to their feelings. Instead, we overbearingly make demands and say foolish things that are unfair and uncalled for, and the children respond in anger— despite their wanting to obey and honor us.

When Saul asked Jonathan for David's whereabouts, he replied, "he is not here. He is gone." However, when Saul began to rebuke Jonathan, he became indignant towards his father and walked away. Here is an example of a father who provoked his child. I think we who have been taught and schooled can take the chain of command and twist it. Fathers can do the same, and take chains of command and twist it for their own benefit.

Let us then also recognize areas where we may be letting anger get out of control. Let's examine ourselves to find out just how much influence unjustified anger has had on our lives. The first area is when anger comes from the wrong motive. There are any number of flimsy motives that can ignite the wrong kind of anger, and one type is jealousy. In Luke 15 we find a familiar story with a less familiar character who depicts jealous anger. As we enter the scene, a welcome home party is in progress for a prodigal son who has just returned. The older brother indicated to the father, "he is not my brother but your son." The older brother's jealous anger had already begun to burn bridges between himself and his younger brother. That same kind of anger can cause friction in us as well; such as when another person receives some kind of commendation, promotion, or attention, which we feel we deserve. The thing we have to ask ourselves when our anger begins to spark, is why am I at this moment getting angry? What is my motive? Is it jealousy? pride? revenge? With the Holy Spirit's help, we can discover the root of our anger and deal with it before it starts to burn out of control.

Secondly, we get angry when things don't go our way. It seems that when things don't go our way, what usually comes our way is a testy, unjustified anger— similar to one that visited Jonah. God had commissioned Jonah, who was a reluctant prophet, to preach to the city of Nineveh. However, Jonah wanted God to destroy those people instead of offering them any chance of repentance. In the end, the stubborn evangelist did preach God's message and the entire city repented and rejoiced— while Jonah fumed. Jonah did not get the destruction he had wanted and he was furious. So he stormed away from God, built himself a shelter, and sat down to pout. Jonah was consumed with the kind of anger we often feel when we get a flat tire. When people on the highway are not driving to suit us, or when it rains on the day we are going to Disney World, underneath our muttering is an attitude of "I've got my rights. I have a right to a perfectly smooth trip. I have a right to a clear lane when I am in a hurry. I have a right to a sunny day whenever I want to be outdoors."

We can sound pretty ridiculous when we strip away the anger that hides our selfish demands. Maybe the ridiculousness can save us from blowing our tops. A joyful heart is good medicine says Proverbs 17:22, and laughter can make all the difference in the world. Seeing the humor in a situation is one of the best ways to handle it when we don't get our way. It's our choice: either we can learn to laugh at ourselves, or we can live on the edge of anger twenty-four hours a day.

Then the final way anger is unjustified is when we react too quickly. When we fly off the handle without investigating the facts, we are sinning— according to the counsel of Solomon and of the Apostle James, although these two lived centuries apart. Ecclesiastes 7:8-9 says the end of a matter is better than the beginning. "Patience of spirit is better than haughtiness of spirit." Do not be eager in your heart to be angry, for anger resides in the bosom of fools. James 1:19 suggests "but let everyone be quick to hear, slow to speak, and slow to anger."

Many of us live on the brink of irritation because we are caught up in the fast pace of this world. Our over-committed schedules drive us through the day in a frenzied pace that prompt us to hear only half of what the other person is saying before we respond, and like a half-cocked pistol, just a little pressure on the trigger is enough to set us off. The best way to disarm this volatile reaction is to cultivate the art of quietness. It is amazing how much more patient and tolerant we become when things are quiet around us. A good way to start doing this is to turn off the noise makers in our lives for a while such as the radio, for instance, and especially the television. The weaning process may be difficult but without the vital practice of solitude and quietness, we will never become mature men and women of God.

What advice does God give us in dealing with anger? There are five points and they are all in the Book of Proverbs. Proverbs 19:11 admonishes us to ignore petty disagreements. "A man's discretion makes him slow to anger, and it is his glory to overlook a transgression or offense." In God's eyes it is a glory if we are big enough to overlook an offense. Some people are so small that they can remember every offense that a person has done against them. To live under those offenses we must be even smaller than the offenses to fit. This verse says it is a glory in God's eyes for us to overlook a matter that is an offense. Therefore, don't look for a fight. As Christians, we are called to keep the chip off our shoulders. We don't have to get defensive about our Savior. We don't have to be defensive about our point to be right, rather be willing to give. That is where God comes in and says that He is able to handle this. We will emerge stronger if we allow some issues to die. Give up, don't tangle because it takes two to quarrel. If we don't participate in the quarrel, then there won't be one. If you see there is an angry disagreement brewing, back off and leave it alone. We should learn to ignore differences that are petty. If there is a principle at stake that's different; however, more often than not it is only our pride that is at stake and so we don't want to miss having the last word.

Another piece of advice in Proverbs 22:24 is to refrain from close association with angry people. Don't hang around them. Do not associate with a person given to anger, or go with a hot-tempered person lest you learn that person's ways and find a snare for yourself. This is an excellent verse to commit to memory. It is true that we become like those with whom we spend our time. If we spend our time with a lustful person we become lustful. If we spend time with a rebel then we become rebellious. We want to be accepted by those with whom we are closely associated, so we tend to adapt each other's ways. The Scripture says if we don't watch it, we will learn the lifestyle of anger from those who are angry. It is true that if we hang around people who are negative then we become negative, and the line of thinking is this won't work or that can't work - which constantly creates doubts. Perhaps many of us are becoming angry because we hang around angry people. Well, the Scripture advises that we don't do it.

The third rule comes from Proverbs 15:1 and suggests that we keep a close check on our tongues. I think there is nothing that breaks up a church quicker than a tongue that is not kept in check. The longer I live, the more I realize this. A gentle anger turns away wrath, but a harsh word stirs up anger. This is a promise! Proverbs 21:23 reads "He who guards his mouth and his tongue guards his soul from trouble." Washington Irving once said "the only tool that gets sharper with use is the tongue." It isn't the muscle in the leg that is the strongest, but it is the muscle in the mouth. We can do far more destruction with what we say than who we kick. This is where Satan wants to win the victory. It takes place once we leave church. The acid test of Sunday service is Monday activity. What do we plan to do with God's help concerning the tongue? If nothing, then we can forget having victory. We must think before we speak. If we do not guard our mouth or tongue, then our soul will experience troubles.

The fourth piece of advice comes from Proverbs 26:6 which instructs us to cultivate honesty in communication without letting anger build up. In Proverbs 27, "wrath is fierce and anger is a flood, but who can stand before jealousy? Open rebuke is better than love that is concealed. Faithful are the wounds of a friend, but deceitful are the kisses of an enemy." If we have something against someone, it should be communicated in love. The result may not be what we want but it needs to be shared. The most effective rebuke I've received has come from those in the body of Christ. Whenever necessary, they did not let the anger build up, for bitter feelings fester as the feelings are held within.

The fifth and final piece of advice is if anger is not controlled it will destroy us. Proverbs 25:28 reads "like a city that is broken down and without walls is a man who has no control over his spirit." This could appeal to lust, pride, and anger. Scripture describes us as fools when we allow anger to run unchecked. Our testimony is at stake when we are involved in negative activity. It isn't worth it to have a business or work if we cannot keep control of our emotions, living on the edge of our emotions. The challenge is to change our office, our business, or change our hearts. In the gospel of Mark, chapter 4, in the parable which Jesus tells about sowing seeds, He warns that Satan comes immediately and takes away the Word. "Immediately" is the key word because even before this day is over Satan will get some of us angry. He wants to take away the good Word that is to be sown.

Some of us are out of balance because our lives are characterized by only the first command of Ephesians 4, "Be angry." Yet others learn to lean totally to the other side to "do not sin," thinking that righteous living has no place for anger. Realistically, both unrestrained anger and the denial of anger will tip the scales towards unrighteousness. There is a proper balance, however, between the two halves. It can be brought about by the exercise of our will, which stands in the gap between "Be angry" and "do not sin."

CHAPTER FIVE

THE WEARINESS OF WORRY

As I look out over the congregation from Sunday to Sunday, I must confess that I do not see anyone who looks worried. We sing wonderfully in praise, most of us usually look comfortable, and we smile in service. So, it may be that this topic of worry would not fit all of us. However, the longer I live the more I realize that if we were able to look down into the real depth of a person's soul, we may find— in the secret chambers where no one knows the thoughts— someone faced with the turmoil of worry. As a matter of fact, Proverbs 14:13 says, "Keep my vision clear." When it comes to this matter of laughing, smiling, and looking as though one is happy, it says that even in laughter, the heart may be in pain, and the end of joy may be grief.

There are real pains even in the heart of one who may be laughing. The preliminaries of a worship service, before the sharing of the Word, prepare us as much as possible by ministering to us in the outward realm. But when God's Word is opened, that is when we get to probe into those feelings where we might find a few worries.

Now whatever the particulars may be, our worries fall under one of three categories. First, there is worry about death, which usually brings feelings of fear and naturally connected with worry. The problems of physical death is one coming to terms with their own or that of a loved one. Some of you may have just received some bad news about your physical self and it looks bleak; or perhaps it is news about a loved one, and there may come a fear regarding their death. If one does not have the Lord Jesus, they have every reason to be afraid. However, if you know Christ you have no reason to be afraid of death. Nevertheless, some of you may be dealing with that fear because of an actual death or fear of death.

The second area is that of disobedience— sin. This brings about feelings of guilt that lead to worry. Something we have done in the past, a realm of our experience that leads us into sin or a number of sins. Even though we have confessed them, we still wrestle with the worry brought about by the guilt. More than likely— in the majority of cases— most of us worry about daily problems: people problems, decision problems, problems related to our jobs or home, problems related to the opposite sex, problems related to finances, and even worries concerning school. I have a worry when it comes to dentists, and I do everything to refrain from going to see my dentist. Maybe you have a worry related to some simple daily problem that eats away at you like a rat in the corner of your life. Maybe your issue is greater than a dentist visit. It could be a foolish mistake you have made that you are paying for now, or it may be a series of foolish mistakes and you are dealing with the consequences.

In the gospel according to Matthew, we are going to examine the middle of Jesus' Sermon on the Mount in chapter 6:25-34. If we were to examine a concordance, we would notice the word "worry" would not be listed because that word, as it appears in our English language, does not occur in the King James Bible. Never do we come across the word worry, and only infrequently is it found in other translations of Scripture. However, there are other terms used besides worry. You will find such words as anxiety, care, trouble, and concern. All of these words fit the concept of worry. So, now in Matthew 6, we have the term "being anxious." Jesus, in verses 25-34, used the word anxious no less than six different times. Since this word is used at least six times, we should want to know what it means. The word literally means to be divided or distracted. It is used most often in the New Testament for something that is divided or distracted. It conveys the idea of being so mentally unerased that we are distracted. We cannot do what we are doing with ease because we are divided in our thinking. The worry or anxiety is pulling our minds towards it, so we cannot give ourselves completely to it nor to the thing we are doing.

A perfect illustration is in Luke 10:38, giving the story of Mary and Martha. Here we find Martha distracted, and Jesus told her that she is bothered by so many things when only a few are necessary. I was reading a Scottish commentary on this verse, and he suggested that the one thing Jesus spoke about in the passage meant one dish. Perhaps Jesus meant for Martha to serve a simple dish like a bowl of cereal so that they could make the most of their time together. But Martha was too distracted, worried, and disturbed. That is the word Jesus uses six times in Matthew's gospel. Now, in this verse 24, the word anxious means to be mentally distracted to the point of being agitated. The phrase that captures our thoughts in this passage is "you cannot serve God and Mammon." You cannot serve God and the power of money. If we commit ourselves to one, we cannot at the same time commit ourselves to the other. Since we try to serve both at the same time, worry will assault or attack us. You can be sure that once you commit yourself to a life of faith and obedience, worry will come in like a flood. Therefore, Jesus gives us five arguments against worry.

The first argument is that worry keeps you from enjoying what you have. Life is more than food, the body is more than clothing. But when we worry we are so occupied with what we don't have that we never enjoy what we have. Isn't life more than these things that we worry about? Do I mean that a person should not provide for his household? Certainly not! The Lord makes it clear that if we do not provide for our household, we are worse than an infidel. What then is the balance? It is simply that worry is the assuming of responsibilities that we cannot handle. It is assuming responsibilities which God never intended for us to handle. God intends for us to make a living. He intends for us to provide for our families, and when we do this God says, "I will meet your needs." He does not say, "I will meet your greed." So, even though we have responsibilities and do our jobs, then the things which we cannot handle should be left alone. For if we occupy our time with worrying, then we will not enjoy what we have presently.

I have read the biography of Thomas Carlye, a great historian and writer. When he built his home in London, he had a chamber which was sound proof, so that he would not be disturbed by outside noises that would distract him from thinking and writing. He had a neighbor who owned a rooster whose sound would penetrate through the wall. Carlye despised this rooster, and he brought this disturbance to his neighbor's attention. To no avail, the owner ignored him. Carlye angrily told the neighbor, "You don't realize what happens when I wait for the rooster to crow. I go through the longest period of waiting— wondering whether it will crow sooner or later— that I could not enjoy the peace and quiet because I became preoccupied with the rooster next door." You may realize that worry can keep us from enjoying what we have at the present time.

The second argument is that worry makes us forget our self-worth. It makes us feel worthless, forgotten, and unimportant; yet Jesus says we are worth much more than those birds who never die of hunger, ulcers, or heart attack because of disturbance or agitation. The point Jesus is making is if God is able to sustain the lesser creature, won't He sustain the greater as well? Some of us are troubled or worried about that which is essential in our lives. Yet, there is no doubt that God knows what is essential better than we know. The things we think are of paramount importance because the needs have not been met, may not be that important after all. We are worth so much that God is taking things one at a time, dealing with more important issues right now in our lives.

The third argument points out that worry is completely useless, for it solves nothing. This is a good time to pause and ask, do you know why you worry? Do you have a deep, respectable love for worry? Do you love it? Do you enjoy it? Note that when one worry is gone, we tend to replace it with another. There is always a line of worry waiting to get into the door, and apparently we enjoy entertaining it. Jesus said that it is worthless. We go to bed and worry why we are only 5'9" and not 5'11" —when we need to realize that this worry will never make us stretch. In reading verse 28, we should bend down to look at the flowers, they are filled with lessons. Worry erases the promise of God from our minds. "Oh, me of little faith— what am I going to do, eat, or wear?" The promise of God is that He will not allow His children to beg bread. God will care for everyone's needs, and that is a promise we can claim. If God took care of the greatest thing on Calvary, then everything else must be less. God will certainly take care of the lesser.

Fourthly, Romans 8:31-32 has a promise from God. "If God is for us, who can be against us." If God gave us Christ on Calvary, how will He not give us all things. This is an encouraging truth. If you are in school, facing a difficult period, assignments are piling up, and the discipline of study is getting old; if you are busy engaged in raising a young family or your family is almost gone and you are alone now without a mate —in either case— the tendency is to worry about what to do next. The worry erases from our minds the fact that God cares, He understands, and God will take care of us.

Note verse 32, which has the strongest rebuke of all. The fifth argument is that worry is a characteristic of the unsaved, not the Christian. Worry is for the person on the street who does not have a personal relationship with God and cares little for the things of God. Worry characterizes such a person and rightfully so, for what else can the individual lean on? However, for the one who is in a relationship with God, He knows that you need to eat, do, and be clothed. God knows, God feeds, and God clothes - not the birds, not the Gentile, not the heathen. Our Father knows we have these needs, and He will not leave us with our needs unmet. As I mentioned earlier, worry is the assumption of a responsibility which was never yours to undertake.

Let's now use God's Word to make a number of practical applications. The first principle is to put your mind first on the Lord. When worry knocks on the door and asks to come in, "seek first His Kingdom and His righteousness, and all these thins that would worry us will be added. Set your mind, first on Him. This is going to make the difference. When temptation first comes to your attention, the tendency is to entertain it with hospitality and let it on to the front porch. It has visited so many times past, and before you realize, it has become a permanent resident. The tendency to let worry in must be stopped. Therefore, seek first God's kingdom and God's will.

The second principle is to remember to live one day at a time. Do not be anxious for tomorrow, for tomorrow will worry about itself. Each day has enough trouble of its own. Why do you want to take on worry on credit? Isn't it bad enough to pay for it now? Try to live one day at a time. Listen to what Robert Berdett wrote: "There are two days in the week on which I never worry. These are carefree days, kept sacredly free from fear and apprehension. One of those days is yesterday and the other day is tomorrow. It isn't the experience of today that drives men mad, but it is the remorse of something that happened yesterday and the dread of what tomorrow may disclose."

That is a scriptural principle which he has put into his own words. We pile up enough worries just for today. Genesis 12 has a family that was filled with worries. We give birth to worries and then we train them in the fine art of how to worry. Here is a man that did just that. His name was Abraham. Worry is not only a sin, but it is deceptive in that we believe we can get better at it. If we develop our worry well enough, we can become one of the top worriers in the world. Abraham was one of the finest worriers there ever was, although he was a great friend of God. God had already promised Abraham that he should have a son through Sarah, and that through Isaac all the families of the earth would be blessed. This was God's promise. This meant Abraham would not die until he had a son, and that Sarah would be the mother of the child. Now Abraham had a test. A famine came into the land, and he began to sojourn there. Abraham began to worry and he told Sarah, "when the Egyptians discover that you are my wife, they will kill me." As you read this, where is Abraham's focus? On himself, obviously. So, in his thinking, he had to plan a strategy. God had already told him he would have Sarah until Isaac was born; therefore, nothing will happen. However, worry erases these promises.

Worry has plans that no one will believe. Abraham told Sarah to say that she was his sister, which was actually a half truth— but we know that half truths are nothing more than dirty lies. So as you can see, Abraham is still focused on himself. For a brief moment, worry pays off as Abraham's life was spared. But God struck Pharaoh's household with a plague because of Abraham's deception and therefore, he was dismissed by Pharaoh. Can you imagine the testimony that Abraham had with Pharaoh who would say, "you say you are a believer in God and yet you lied to me?" We would think that Abraham learned his lesson. However, in Genesis 20, he does the same thing again. So you see, worry is like that and if we actually become skilled at it to the point it comes almost natural after awhile. In Genesis 26:6, we see that the worry has passed from father to son. Isaac lied about Rebecca because he was afraid that the village would kill him. Even his grandson, Jacob, became a worrier. He cheated his brother out of his own birth right, and when it finally caught up with him, the law of diminishing return took hold. When he realized that Esau was coming towards him, he prayed (Genesis 31:32) that God would spare his life. Notice that worry knocks on our door right after we knock to speak with God in prayer. We pour out our hearts saying, "Lord, take this need and I'm not going to worry about it." At the conclusion of our prayers we take it back from God and decide to live with worry some more.

So, what do we do in the final analysis when worry comes? Let me conclude with four simple words. How do we handle worry?

Presence: Claim God's presence. The first thing we should say to ourselves is, "I'm not alone." Read verses from Isaiah 40:10, Joshua 1:9, Matthew 28:20 in order to strengthen your faith in God's presence.

Promise: Get into the Word and discover God's promises. Someone counted and found that there are 7,474 promises in Scripture. That is definitely enough to keep us busy for a long while. Discover some of God's promises on your own and hold on to them when problems attack.

In Isaiah 26:3-4, "Thou will keep him in perfect peace whose mind is stayed on Thee."

Psalm 37:4-5, "Delight thyself also in the Lord and He shall give you the desires of your heart. Commit thy way unto the Lord, trust also in Him and He shall bring it to past."

So, thus far you see that there's no need to worry when you have God's presence, for He is with you. God's promises have been given for you to claim. If you have problems with insomnia, read Psalm 4:8, "I will lay me down and sleep, lay down in peace because Thou, O Lord, let me dwell in safety."

Prayer: Lifting specific prayer in which you name the issues to God.

Phil. 4:6-7, Stop worrying about everything; "Be anxious for nothing but in everything by prayer and supplication, with thanksgiving, let your requests be made known unto God, and the peace of God that passeth all understanding shall march guard duty around your heart."

I Peter 5:7, "Cast all your cares upon Him for He cares for you."

Psalm 55:22, "Roll your burden on the Lord and He will sustain you. He will never suffer the righteous to be moved." Dump your burdens on the Lord. Don't walk around with it on your back, leave it with Him.

Patience: In Isaiah 40:31, "They that wait on the Lord shall renew their strength."

Romans 8:25, "If we hope for that which we see not, then we wait in patience for it."

Psalm 27:14, "Wait on the Lord and He shall strengthen thy heart. Wait, I say, on the Lord."

If you have an illness and try to diagnose it on your own, you find out that you cannot do so. So you go to the doctor for an examination of your eyes, heart, throat, pulse, etc., and you get a complete check-up before he/she gives you the diagnosis. Then when the doctor writes the prescription, you refuse to take it and instead remain sick— but you complain about it. The doctor tells you not to call back unless you have tried the pills. Though you may be offended, the doctor has right to respond in that way, because it is in ignorance you say that the prescription would not work for you. Well, that is exactly what Satan wants you to say about how you handle your worries. Now that you have completed this chapter, Satan wants you to say, "those are nice prescriptive verses, but they won't work for me." I challenge you to try these prescriptions, and don't let Satan sell you short and steal the victory that should be yours.

CHAPTER SIX

WHEN LONELINESS LINGERS

If I were to ask you to describe someone who is lonely, chances are you would not choose someone who is busy. It is also doubtful that you would select someone in a top management position, such as the chief executive officer in a growing corporation, or the leading, well-paid salesperson in an aggressive, competitive organization. Of course, our thought is, "Not them! They are successful. They have money. They are fulfilled. They haven't the time to be lonely." Well, don't bet on it. Loneliness is the plague of the loner— and, by and large, "top dogs" are loners. Contentment is seldom found in the penthouse. Instead, there is boredom and stark feelings of emptiness. These are people who lead lives of quiet desperation.

Loneliness has been called the most desolate condition in the world. If you have been lonely, you know this to be true. It is probable that most people are not lonely as we normally think of the word "lonely," but it is also quite possible that some of you are truly lonely.

It is certainly true that all of us have experienced at some time or another the desolate feeling of being lonely. I think of a dear widow, who lived for thirty years in marital bliss with her husband, and suddenly without announcement God took him from her side. That widow lived the rest of her days consumed by the spell of loneliness. She told me that I could not really fully understand the ache of her life because I still have my mate, and she was right. Being that I had not lived thirty years in bliss with one and being that I was in love, I had no idea what it was like to come home in the evening to fix a meal for one, to set the table for one, to clean up dishes after one, or to look across the table at the chair that was once occupied by a beloved and around the table at the chairs which were once occupied by family. And— now— there is only one.

I think about a young woman who was in my first church. A very attractive individual, a registered nurse who was extremely lonely on the inside. She was a beautiful person who had fallen in love and had come to New York to become better acquainted with her fiancé and ultimately get married. Suddenly the romance took a wrong turn and was fractured, being later destroyed. The young woman made plans to return South to her home. As she told me her story, I wrote down one of her specific comments, "neither an excellent job nor a sound, friendly church can remove the lonely ache of my heart. I am going home more lonely than I've ever dreamed possible." Here is a person who has all the promise and beauty anyone would want, yet she sees only loneliness in her future. Loneliness is not confined to our land or just to people in church, or just to widows. It affects the divorcee, the prison inmate, the aged, those who are as strangers in their area and don't know anyone around them. It affects the college student away from home, or the one who has gotten into trouble. Loneliness knows no barriers and is not gentle with anyone, but rather it invades the life of most anyone.

In II Timothy 4, there is one of the most aching and desolate experiences of the word "lonely." This lonely passage depicts Paul's situation as such, that even the great apostle himself could not shake the loneliness of that moment. Let me explain why. This is his last written piece of communication. II Timothy is the last epistle which Paul wrote. The events that lead him to the writing of this chapter are too lengthy and complex to go into at this moment; but, it will suffice to say that the chain of events which lead up to this moment was desperate. His life is now at stake and he has come to the end of a rich, full, rewarding and persecuted life.

The first reason Paul was lonely is his location. He was in a dungeon. It is difficult to appreciate certain passages if we fail to identify with the circumstances of the writer. This passage was not written from a pastor's study or quiet hilltop or a log cabin tucked away in New England. It was written from a dungeon in the Mamertime Prison in Rome. This was Paul's last place before his death, so his situation was depressing and lonely. A second reason for Paul's loneliness was that he was all alone. He didn't have anybody around him in that dungeon. Look at verse 9. He begged Timothy to come to see him soon. Everyone had left him. He was not familiar with anyone around him except Dr. Luke.

This could be the situation which some of us are facing. We live in places where we do not know anyone or only a few people, and we even feel like asking, "Where is God? Where is this thing they call fellowship, friendship, and love?" Paul was lonely because he was in a dungeon, alone.

The third reason Paul was lonely in verse 21 was that winter was just around the corner. This verse is filled with emotions. Carl McCarthy, the great preacher for the Presbyterian Church, delivered a sermon entitled "Come Before Winter." There are certain seasons of the year that lend itself to loneliness. Winter is one of these seasons. The lingering fall gives way to a lengthy winter season. So Paul told Timothy to come, but do so before winter. There is a popular song which says, "None but the lonely heart can feel the anguish..." If you have never been alone throughout a winter, you cannot appreciate the loneliness of Paul's heart. We have the highest attempted suicide rate in the winter. There is something about the cold months that lends itself to loneliness.

There was yet another factor worse than winter for Paul's loneliness, and that was the fact that death was near. (If you look back at verse 6, Paul faced the reality of his death.) Paul's demise was only weakening. Therefore, he was filled with memories as indicated in verse 16. Understandably so, Paul became very emotional when he stood before the court of Rome and he looked around for any defenders. But there were no witnesses in his favor.

Isn't this funny how our feelings— certain smells, sights, certain scenes or spending time with certain persons— puts us in nostalgia? I remember my first serious case of working with suicide. I entered the man's home and the walls were lined with pictures of his son. He began to tell me the sad story of his past. He had lost his health, his wife and his son. All he had to turn to were these photographs. He had all of the experiences of his son only captured in pictures. That same evening, he took his life because he was desperately lonely.

I wish I could say that once we come to Christ we would never experience loneliness again. But those of you who know the Lord and are still lonely would call me a liar. In Hebrews 11, there is recorded the greatest role call of the Bible. Hebrews 11:35 records the fact that even the devoted and godly go through desperate and lonely times. So keep in mind that when we experience loneliness, we are in good company. These people had their lives taken from them and God has allowed us to live through our experiences, perhaps so that we may get some help on how to cure those feelings of loneliness. Therefore, let us look at some of the cures.

Paul had every reason to be lonely. He was in a dungeon, all alone, winter was coming, death was near, and nostalgic memories swamped him. What did he do about it? There were four things that Paul requested. In those four requests we have some answers to dealing with loneliness. First, Paul requested companionship. In verse 9, he told Timothy to make every effort to come to him soon. There is a sense of urgency for Timothy to come before wintertime— in short, Paul insisted, "Come quick and pick up John Mark on your way." If you consider this closely, you will see that this statement is filled with meaning.

The story of John Mark is out of the picturesque part of the New Testament. A missionary defector who said in days past when times became difficult, "I want to go back home," and Paul told him to go. However, when Paul decided to make a second journey and Mark wanted to go along, Paul and Barnabas became incensed over this issue and consequently separated in their work. Barnabas took Mark, and Paul took Silas.

Paul, now at the end of his life, told Timothy, "When you come, bring John Mark. Mark has something that will profit me in the ministry." Some of us believe we do not need anyone, but the time will come when death awaits us, and then we will realize that we do need others. Paul was a brave man, but let's notice how at the end of his life he says to "bring Mark." Notice that he didn't say bring everyone; rather, he picks the people he wants to spend time with. This is something which is perfectly fine when you are lonely because you don't want/need the entire church there. We should want only a selected list of people. Paul requests Timothy, Luke and Mark to be there in his loneliness.

When we are lonely and the devil tempts us with depressing thoughts, we need to make an effort towards companionship with specifically chosen people who will minister to us. The streams of loneliness are fed by the streams of isolation. When we have those feelings of isolation, we should pick specific individuals and tell them to come and spend some time together— let's encourage each other. In order for us to ask someone to come, we have to reach out and admit that we have weaknesses. We don't like to do this, but if we are big enough to admit our weaknesses, we are far along in our Christian walk. So we see, Paul said to Timothy: bring Mark and come quick because I need you now.

In verse 13, Paul asks for something else. He asks for bodily comfort. He tells Timothy when you come, bring the cloak which I left at Troas with Carpus. What did he request? — a cloak. It was cold and damp in the dungeon, and winter was approaching. It was uncomfortable, and Paul was not willing to die an early death by not taking care of himself. So he said there are some things that I need in order to stay comfortable. Paul wanted this specific cloak which was left in Troas with Carpus. I can picture the history of this cloak vividly in my mind. It is probably that this was the cloak which he had on when Stephen was murdered. It had been yellowed from shipwreck. It had been red from blood when he was stoned at Lystra; white from snow at Pamphylia and Galatia. This cloak is probably rich in history. So I can understand why Paul said, "When you come Timothy, bring that cloak." I can imagine that when the cloak was brought to him he put it on, and he remembered the pleasure and pain of the years. It's meaningful to him in that moment of need.

Fifteen hundred years later, Winston Tisdale made a similar request. He asked for some leggings to keep his legs warm and a cloak to warm his body, as he studied the Bible in that prison in his last days. After we seek companionship, we have to take care of ourselves. Sometimes when we lose a mate, we have the feeling that life is not worth living. Therefore, once this becomes evident we fail to take care of ourselves. As loneliness gets worse, our bodily condition gets worse. Because we lose part of our health, we then become victims of our own needs. Let's learn a lesson from Paul when he told Timothy to pay attention to yourself and teachings. Take care of yourself for you have a job to do. Paul took care of himself. Loneliness is lessened when we keep our bodies in shape.

Next, the request was to bring the books. Here is an itinerant missionary who has a library. Timothy knew where these books were. These weren't the books of the Bible, these are the ancient writings that ministered to the minds of the apostle Paul. Paul did not want to waste away in the dungeon, not using his mind. He wanted to continue to read and expand himself. He was not pressed out of panic because he had to study. He loved to read because it was stimulating to him. So he said to Timothy please bring the book. Charles Spurgeon said in order for us to be able to expound the Scriptures and as an aid to our pulpit, we must read the commentary. Expand your library! In your growing, in your getting older, continue to read and expand your knowledge. Don't neglect the ancient— there is more than a night at the movies, or a nine o'clock television show; more than a sports game and a newspaper; there is even more than the computer— there are books longing to be read that will broaden and deepen our lives. Be widely and wisely read. We should force ourselves to read, and it's amazing what it will do to our loneliness. If we cannot take the trip, the books will help us make the journey. Therefore, companionship is important; bodily comfort is essential; the reading of good books will broaden us and make us forget ourselves.

Finally, "Bring the parchments." That was Paul's personal copy of the Old Testament Scriptures and part of the New Testament that were being compiled. Why, Paul? "I need to spend time in the Word." I appreciate the various translations of the Scriptures and so often we read and need clarity, and it is only then that we can reach for our own Bible— which should be well-marked, underlined, circled, torn, frayed, ragged— and we are familiar with it. Timothy, when you come bring the parchments. Paul was lost in the Word of God, for it was his companion both night and day.

Loneliness has a way of winning the victory. Oh, how I wish it could be defeated, that cursed enemy. We cannot be immune to it, but we can gain the victory over it. I suggest four ways of dealing with loneliness.

☐ Seek out some close friends.

☐ Keep yourself in good shape./Take care of your needs.

☐ Expand your mind by reading good, challenging books.

☐ Get into the Word of God personally on a regular basis.

If you do not know Christ, I have no solution for your loneliness. You can have close friends, be in fine shape, be the widest read person around, and even have knowledge of Scripture— but when you turn that light off and put your head on that pillow, you will be still be lonely— because you do not have a Savior. Please do not let God chase you any longer. We have neglected the God of the universe. His name shall be called Emmanuel— God with us. He is the Mighty Counselor.

CHAPTER SEVEN

THE INSANITY OF INFERIORITY

I think it is an interesting contrast when we realize that there is enough atomic power in one human body to destroy the City of New York. I was talking with a brilliant man of science, and I remember his comment about the power of the human mind. He said, "it's almost impossible to figure this out, but if we could build an electronic computer that could do all the mind can do, it would be a building about a city block wide and deep and be about twenty-two stories high. The power of the body and the power of the mind in the human being today is nothing short of phenomenal." Yet, it is amazing in contrast to this how many people coward in timidity and inferiority.

There are three things which need to be said before we look at the lives of three men— two of whom faced the problem of inferiority and did not seem to conquer it easily, and the other who could have had the problem but did not, for he knew how to handle it. First, inferiority is not related to intelligence. When we observe the writings or histories of those who are highly intelligent, they suffer from more inferior feelings than those beneath that mark, for those who have relatively lower intelligence quota have relatively little inferiority. Therefore, inferiority is not necessarily related to a low or high IQ The second thing I found interesting was that inferiority was not always noticed on the surface. More than likely we mask it in a number of interesting ways. There are many compensations which people use to cover up their inferiority. One common mask is the personality which we call the Superiority Complex— the boisterous type of personality that is always on top of things, and the impression is that one would not expect inferiority from such persons. Another mask is sarcasm. Many people we know have strong tendencies towards sarcasm, and often that is a cover up or compensation for their inferiority. The third issue of inferiority is that Christians wrestle with this problem just as much as non-Christians. We wrestle with it deeply, and it is not always obvious on the surface. People may find comfort in their work, but behind the scene there is this problem. Many people suffer from feelings of a deep sense of unworthiness, acute inadequacy, lack of confidence and an inability to accept themselves. In today's market, the commodities of beauty, intelligence and wealth pay the highest dividends of conferred worth. Without them, we are made to feel we are something less than we should be. We are harangued daily by society's built-in slant which rewards the "haves" and punishes the "have-nots." In this brutal, cultural milieu of the survival of the worthiest, the less gifted attempt to survive by trying to compensate through over-achievement, superiority, and other negative behaviors. Yet, despite our best efforts to clothe ourselves with worth, underneath it all is the parasite of inferiority which still feeds on our souls. Inferiority is a parasite of sin that feeds off our separation from God. It first became attached to mankind through the act of rebellion in the Garden, and since then it has gorged itself on the unstable substitutes for God that people rely on for worthiness.

In this chapter, we want to turn to the timeless counsel of the Bible and reach for God's help in dealing with the painful problem of inferiority. Let's go back in time and look at a young man at 80 years of age in Exodus Chapter 3. This is a person whom we would not suspect to be suffering from inferiority feelings, but Moses certainly did. The reason he felt inferior was that he had a background of failure, and guilt frequently brings on inferiority whether it is created by something that one has done, or something which one feels can never be made right. So Moses lived out his life with that weight of failure weighing heavily on his shoulder. That is how we discover Moses in Exodus 3. He had murdered a man in Egypt and was sent from Egypt back to an unknown area known as the Midian desert, a place of obscurity, where he lived with his father and mother-in-law. There he was forgotten, now 80 years old, and for forty years he was not seen by the public. When Moses was called, challenged and commissioned by God to go tell Pharaoh to let God's people go, all of Moses' failures appeared before his eyes and he felt inferior to the task. In verse 11, Moses questioned God by saying, "I cannot go because I do not feel qualified," and he refused to accept the initial challenge. In Chapter 4, verse 1, Moses became self-focused and God had to demonstrate His power to convince Moses that by His power he would be guided throughout the encounter with Pharaoh. Moses continued to display feelings of insecurity by appealing to his inadequate public speaking skills.

So many people can identify with Moses in verse 10. How frequently one hears from others about their lack of proper speaking skills. Here is Moses saying, "I am not eloquent," and God rebukes him by saying, "I will take the responsibility for your tongue." God promised Moses to take his inability and give him the words to say. If we feel inferior with our words, God is able to handle that inability and turn what seems to be a restraint or barrier into a blessing, even if it is for nothing more than to keep us trusting from word to word in order for God to give us the words to say. It is interesting to note that Moses took Aaron, his brother, to be a mouthpiece who became the very one that would be responsible for that golden calf at the bottom of Sinai. Moses must have been pricked in his heart when he thought he could have done the job before God and did not have to lead the people in that way. Here is the example of the person who felt inferior, but God did not give up on Moses. Moses vividly mirrors the truth that how we view ourselves will affect how we interpret everything around us. It explains how we may look straight into the brilliance of the morning sun and see only darkness; how God's fiery presence was only inches away, yet all Moses could see was the blackness of his own inadequacies.

Now, let's examine the life of Jeremiah. We have the idea that these prophets of God never suffered from inferiority, and never felt inadequate. Jeremiah certainly did. In the first chapter of this book (verse 4) his inferiority is displayed, using the same line from the life of Moses. "I do not know how to speak." It would seem that as soon as God places His hand on a person whom He declares - the person cries out, "I can't," —as if that be the only way in which God can use people. Jeremiah's excuse was that he was too young and therefore lacked wisdom to speak to the elders of Israel, and he lacked the charisma that would reach them and win them.

It is interesting that we have feelings of inferiority because of the fear of the other person. The marvelous story of verse 9 is that God stretched out His hand and touched Jeremiah's mouth and placed His words also in Jeremiah's mouth. That is not an idle idea, that is a real point. If we are going to speak God's message, He will give us the words to say as we speak His Word. The difference between some speakers of the Gospel is that some believe they have to say something, while others have something to say. God told Jeremiah that he will have something to say and that he will say God's Word.

Before leaving the Old Testament, let's examine a less familiar face— the person of Amos whose faith guarded him against any trace of inferiority. In the book of Amos, we encounter a person who had every reason to feel inferior. He had no formal training in school. He was not attractive, didn't dress well, was not eloquent, nor was he raised in the court like Solomon. However, he had an interesting background. He was a fig picker by occupation. His job was to harvest fruit from sycamore trees, and a picker had the responsibility of mashing the fruit so it would be soft to the buyer. When you crush this fruit it would stain the hands. Amos was both a fig picker and a squeezer.

In Chapter 7 of Amos, he is standing in the courts of the King, and they are eyeing each other as Amos is preaching. Amos is the person whom God chose to represent Him before Amaziah, the priest of Bethel. When the socially polished, beautifully attired, eloquent and unsaved priest hears what Amos has to say, he tells Amos, in no uncertain terms, to get out. However, Amos did not back away. Amos did not look down at his clothes or his stained hands and wonder what in the world is he doing there. Instead, Amos kept his eyes focused on the Lord. He stood firm on the truths God had revealed to him and refused to leave until Amaziah heard them all. The point is so obvious that when our eyes are on ourselves, we will not even get out of our own home if the task is difficult. But if our eyes are fixed on God, we can step into life and God will strengthen us for the task.

Let's get some personal principles, now that we have seen the problem of inferiority illustrated in the lives of Moses, Jeremiah, and Amos. What principles can we gain from the New Testament? The first is the Lord's estimate of us. In Matthew 6:26, Jesus shares a profound truth that can dispel our dark clouds of self-doubt. Verse 26 tells what God thinks about us as His children. "Look at the birds of the air, that they do not sow, neither do they reap, nor gather into barns, and yet your heavenly Father feeds them. Are you not worth much more than they?" We are worth much more to God. Even though the subject of this verse is worry, the point made about our value cannot be missed. If God can handle a little sparrow in the sky and sustain that bird, will God not be all the more concerned about us? God confirms the fact that we are worth much more than grass, lilies, and sparrows. God loves us to the immeasurable extent of sacrificing His Son. Therefore, the next time we think about how pitiful and inferior we feel, remember that to God we are the object of God's attention and affection. If it were not for our need, there would not have been a Savior. In Ephesians 2:10, Paul made the point that God is at work in each of us. We are God's workmanship. God is giving attention to us as individuals. He doesn't look upon the mass of humanity and pick out the body of Christ within that larger mass to shower blessings to just that whole group. God knows each individual and with each one of us He is working. Philippians 1:6 says that God is not through working with us. God, who began working on us, will complete the work in us. The individual who is absorbed in feelings of inferiority thinks he/she is not as good as the next person. What such persons fail to remember is that we are independently being worked on by God. Our eyes continually scan the surface, comparing ourselves with others - yet God just deals with us as individuals, and He is not even near through with us.

According to God, we are very important to Him. This is not just good psychology, this is sound biblical doctrine. God sent His Son for us and is conforming us to the image of His Son. Since God is working on us as unique vessels of God, and since God is not finished with us, we need to consider ourselves, along with God, as a team— rather than seeing ourselves in competition with others. We should think of it all as a cooperative relationship. We are like diamonds in the rough, and God works on us by punching away and striking away, buffing and polishing, and hopefully we are cooperating as our diamond is shaped and prepared for some task and plan which God has for us. The process at times can be irritating, and the one who feels most inferior is the one whose diamond is so rough that he/she gets in the way before that area is completed. God is working on each of our diamonds, and His work is not finished.

The second principle is our worth in the body of Christ. The body of Christ is the entire family of God on earth today. Every living soul around the world who is a born-again believer in Christ is a member of God's body. We are seen in God's Word as a family. Christ is the head and as the body we, as Paul explains in I Corinthians 12, are fingers, arms, knees, toes and even tiny organs which are not apparently visible. However, instead of being content to be the parts which God has designed us to be, we invite inferiority to creep in as we compare ourselves to each other. In Verse 18,

"God has placed the members just as He desires." God made us who we are because that is His desire for us and it pleases Him. Persons who suffer from inferiority are dissatisfied with their design and believe they cannot be useful in the way they were designed. Some organs of the body that we never see are just as important, and if they weren't there the body would suffer. Every person is a vital organ whether seen or unseen in the body. One characteristic of the body is that it cares for all the members. We cannot say my finger hurts, but I feel good everywhere else When one member hurts, we all hurt because we are all important.

The third principle is our personal estimate of ourselves. Romans 12:3 challenges us to be honest about our estimate of ourselves. "For through the grace given to me I say to every person among you not to think more highly of oneself than one ought to be think; but think so as to have sound judgment; as God has allotted to each a measure of faith." With pride as our teacher, we become arrogant and our sense of worth gets over inflated. Whereas, under inferiority's tutelage, we belittle ourselves into thinking we are insignificant to God and other people. But Paul exhorts us to have a sane or sound estimate of ourselves, and we can have such an estimate only as we accept God's view of us.

Let's discuss how we can apply these principles to our everyday lives. First, *we must realize that we were prescribed before birth*. We are all prescription babies. God made us just like He wants us. God made us with the hair color, height, and skin color He wanted. This is frequently a real problem with people who feel inferior. We are not a product of chance but rather a work of art from the mind of God. God has placed His signature on us with the indelible ink of God's image. There is nothing about us or the days of our lives - even before we took our first breath— for we had the loving scrutiny of our heavenly Father, as recorded in Psalm 139:13-16.

Secondly, *remember that the growth process is still going on.* At times, we become frustrated with our slow growth and open the door to self-defeat with thoughts like: "I am no good ... I keep making the same mistakes ... God is probably sick of me." But Paul tells us to hold on, to get our eyes off of ourselves and stay confident in the fact that God is at work in us— even when we don't see it. "For I am confident of this very thing, that He who began a good work in you will perfect it until the day of Christ Jesus." (Phil. 1:6)

Thirdly, *refuse to compare yourself with others.* Stop looking at others and look only at the Lord. II Corinthians 10:5 states, "we are taking every thought captive to the obedience of Christ." Our feelings of inferiority thrive on those renegade thoughts which we allow to pass through our minds uncontested. They can run by so quickly sometimes that we are not even aware of thinking them. To get control of them, we must train ourselves to constantly stand guard at the door of our minds with the truth. Inferiority never rests. It will seize every opportunity which we allow it to continue to brainwash us with its doctrine of worthlessness. It boils down to this: will we submit to the liberating truth of Christ, or will we submit to being held prisoner of the lies of inferiority?

The fourth: *respond correctly to our shortcomings.* We all have defects, scars, or shortcomings that we must learn to deal with. Paul provides us with a personal glimpse in II Corinthians 12:7-9 into how Paul handled one such problem. From this passage we can discuss three things. First, we can feel the freedom to pray to have these things corrected.

Second, if the Lord chooses to leave them with us, we must learn to accept our shortcomings as a way for God to display His power in and through us. Thirdly, Paul points out that the news of shortcomings is not all bad. For it is often in our areas of weakness that we see most clearly the reality of the Savior's work in our lives. Feelings of inferiority that have built up over the years are difficult to overcome. BUT it can be done. We must resist the tendency to place our self-worth and the worth of others according to the same values in which the world buys stock. To do this, we must follow God's advice in Romans 12:2 to renew our minds in God's truth. As a member of the body of Christ, we must help one another sensitively and faithfully apply the God-given truths about our worth.

I have a friend who has a bright, red mark on his face which stretches in an ugly fashion across his nose. But this friend has no difficulty with inferiority. Once I had enough courage to ask him how he could be so effective on his feet and allow God to use him in such a way without wrestling. He explained that his dad taught him that the ugly scar on his face must have been the place where an angel had kissed him before he was born. Apparently, his dad conveyed to him that he was marked out by God because he was unique. His dad told him on a continuous basis that he is the most important person on earth. This friend said that he got to the point where he felt sorry for people who did not have a mark on the side of their face. So you see, this is how one turns a shortcoming unto the glory of God. Until we can do that, we will never conquer the problem of inferiority.

CHAPTER EIGHT

THE DANGERS OF DISCOURAGEMENT

A mother of eight children came home one day to find her youngest five huddled intently in the middle of the yard. She walked over to see what the center of attraction was and discovered that they were playing with five baby skunks. Aghast, she shouted, "Run, children, run!"— and run the children did, each clutching one terrified skunk. Can you imagine five children with skunks, all running in different directions? And the farther each child ran, the louder the mother probably shouted— causing all to panic and squeeze their skunks? Remember, skunks don't like to be squeezed.

All of us have had a problem blow up in our face and end up as a stinking mess. Those situations can knock the wind right out of our confidence and leave us feeling beat and discouraged. And there is nothing quite like dealing with the problem of discouragement when one is in a position of leadership— even if it is only leading five gamely children to a backyard hose.

I suspect that Satan's number one tool is discouragement. If Satan can discourage us, make us want to quit, make us not want to care anymore— if he can get us to any one of these points, then he will control all areas of our lives. If you are human, then you battle this issue of discouragement. If you are hoping for something that may never materialize; wanting a promotion you didn't get; getting a promotion and realize it was not what it was cracked up to be; looking forward to marriage and realize it is more than you can handle; buying that thing you saved up for only to ask yourself what is the big deal: watch out for discouragement! If Satan can discourage us, he can take us on a road to spiritual disaster.

The next lesson we can learn is from Elijah, and that is the lesson of discouragement. Let's look at the battle and the plague of discouragement as we review Chapter 18 of I Kings. I hope you have not forgotten that at this point in the story Elijah is on Mount Carmel. Elijah feels as if he is on top of the world because he was there taunting the god of Baal saying perhaps your god is using the bathroom or on vacation. He was so confident and full of vim, vigor and vitality. He could stand amidst 450 prophets of Baal and 400 prophets of Asherah, and he stood with guts to taunt them and did not bend. Have you had times in your life when you believed no one could whip you, when you felt on top of the world?

In Chapter 18 Elijah prayed, "Lord, show them who is God." He poured water on their sacrifice. The fire came down and licked up their sacrifice, and then he heard thunder and lightening, and God moved wonderfully in him. Once again, Elijah was on top of the world. He had nothing to be afraid of. However, James in the New Testament— when reflecting on Elijah— said, "He was a man of like passion as we are." Up to this point Elijah seemed to be a super prophet. For many of us our envy would be to be like Elijah, but the Bible says Elijah was like us - up one day and down the next.

Let's look at the downside of Elijah, showing he was subject to the same human fragility as we are.

We read in Verse 1 that Elijah was on the run. My man had just killed 850 prophets, called fire down from heaven, outran a horse from Mount Carmel to Jezreel - Elijah was on top of the world. Yet, one little old lady shook this man up so bad, that he ran from her 140 miles from Jezreel down to Beersheba. He was scared. What happened was Ahab came home after witnessing the event which occurred on Mount Carmel. He told his wife what Elijah had done. He said, "Jezebel, you wouldn't believe what Elijah did to our prophets. He killed all of them. That Elijah is something else." Jezebel sent a message to Elijah saying, "By the Baalim if I don't chop your neck off by tomorrow this time, if I don't kill you, may the gods kill me!" Her hatred for Elijah was so much that she was willing to put her own life on the line to see him dead. When Elijah heard this, he got so scared that he decided to leave town. He ran all to the way south to Judah, 140 miles, where he left his servant as a divergent, so that he could go another 50 miles in the desert.

Let me outline at least five principles of discouragement. First of all, discouragement comes in when we forget what God did yesterday because we are looking at our circumstances today. Elijah had just come off Mount Carmel and had seen all the prophets destroyed. He had seen the power of God, but now this women had scared him. He had forgotten what God had done yesterday. One of the reasons we become discouraged is that we forget the God who has brought us to where we are now. We tend to forget somehow the God who lives in the past is also good enough for the present. I want to serve notice that if we are going to be able to overcome the circumstances of today, we cannot leave God on Mount Carmel. We have to bring God down to our

Jezreel. If all we can do is remember, when we go back in history, is how things were yesterday - then a God of yesterday is only good for yesterday. However, unless that God of yesterday on Mount Carmel can get into our today and tomorrow, then discouragement is bound to set in.

Elijah had forgotten that God defeated 850 prophets. He had forgotten that 450 prayed to their god and their god let them down. How often we forget that God brought us through yesterday. Do you remember last week when you didn't think you could make it? But you are here today. Do you remember when you didn't think you could get through this trial, but you got through it? How about when you didn't think you could live another day? But you are here. If God did it yesterday, has He died since then? Don't forget what God did on your Mount Carmel.

The second principle is we never focus on our circumstances, but we should always focus on God. Remember Chapter 17:1-5. Elijah from the tribe of the Tishbite said to Ahab, "As the Lord God of Israel lives, before whom I stand..." What confidence he conveyed to the king - what strength, what internal fortitude! In Chapter 17 verse 13, once again Elijah here said to the woman, "Do not be afraid, but bake a cake for me and God will bless you." What great advice to tell this women not to be afraid. Yet, when it happened to Elijah he said, "I am scared. I have got to get out of town." He focused on his circumstances. If we are going to be able to beat discouragement, then we cannot keep looking in the face of our problem— without, at the same time, looking in the face of our God.

The power over discouragement is when we compare what is bigger— our problem or our God. As long as our Jezebel (problem) looks bigger than God or covers our God that we cannot see Him, then the circumstances will control how we feel. However, if we look at God first and put God in front of our circumstances, everything will fall into the right perspective. Our problem is we focus too much on our circumstances and not on God. That is what happened to Peter when he was walking on the water. He walked on the water, and he looked at the winds and the waves but he took his eyes off Jesus. The circumstances were getting ready to swallow him up because he began to sink. But in the midst of his sinking, he looked up at Jesus and he said, "Lord, save me!" Jesus grabbed him by the hand because he took his eyes off Him. We have to focus on the Lord at times of discouragement. Paul says, "Rejoice in the Lord always and again I say rejoice." Paul was writing this encouragement from prison. Paul says that we should find our chief joy in the Lord. What happens to many of us when we get discouraged is we don't want to hear about the Lord; we have no desire to read the Bible; we have no desire to pray or even attend Bible study.

One of the great tricks of Satan in time of discouragement is to make us believe God is not the answer. We now need a real answer, something that will really work. We believe there is this attitude to rush the pastor to do his/her thing so that the individual can find some real solution. When we can learn to look at our problems through the telescopic eyes of God, what we see that is greater is the God who is in us than he who is in the world. Don't focus on circumstances, just focus on God. Verse 4 says that Elijah sat down under a tree. There he requested that he might die. His cry was, "Lord, take my life! I am no better than my fathers." In reality Elijah was saying, "I quit, and I want to die. Kill me, I am no better than my fathers. I am nothing. My life is not going anywhere."

The third principle is discouragement will make us feel sorry for ourselves and develop self pity. Elijah began to feel sorry for himself. "I am no better than my fathers." What happens when we began to feel sorry for ourselves is that we pray dumb prayers. "Lord, kill me. Lord, let me die. I had enough and I cannot take it any more!" Elijah is lying. He doesn't want to die. If he wanted to die he would not have run. He wanted to live so he ran as far from Jezebel as he could. He felt sorry for himself and he wanted God to feel sorry for him, too. People are like that whenever they feel sorry for themselves. Like Elijah, they want us to feel sorry for them, too. Some of us get miserable just to get attention. For example, a suicide victim's call of desperation is for somebody to listen. He/she is seeking attention. Why do people get drunk in public? Because they are seeking attention.

Elijah wanted divine attention, so he got caught up in self pity. God did not give him what he wanted, he gave him what he needed. Verses 5 & 6 says he ate and went to sleep. God became very practical with Elijah. Sometimes we just need some rest. Elijah was physically exhausted and emotionally spent. His ministry was moving at full speed and his adrenaline had dried up. He was on the verge of burnout. When people get to the point of complete exhaustion, they exhibit certain symptoms. They become irritable, short-tempered and their minds play tricks on them.

What Was God's Response to Elijah?

Instead of rebuking Elijah and making him feel guilty and feel ashamed, God gently picked Elijah up and set him on his feet again. He provided Elijah rest and nourishment. The angel of the Lord tended to Elijah. It is beautiful to see how God, who needs neither sleep nor nourishment, understands the physical needs of God's people. Don't feel guilty when you rest, play and laugh.

Secondly, he communicated wisely with Elijah. God told Elijah, "Arise and eat because the journey is too great for you." He responds by traveling for forty days and forty nights to Mount Horeb in the strength of the food God had given him. The number forty has spiritual significance. Forty is the fire for spiritual preparation. In Old Testament, Israel was in the wilderness for 40 days. The purpose was to prepare them for Canaan. Jesus was in the wilderness for forty days. The purpose was to prepare him through temptation for what was coming. God was concerned about Elijah and asked, "What are you doing here, Elijah?" Elijah said, "I serve you and those people will never do right. That's way I am here." God replied, "Go out and stand before Me." The Scripture tells us "Behold the Lord was passing by." There was strong thunder but God was not in the wind. After the wind, there was earthquake, and God was not in earthquake. Then there was fire, but the Lord was not in the fire. After the fire, there was sound of a soft, gentle blowing. God was in the breeze, and it was then He spoke to Elijah. We should take note that God was not in the storm because sometimes we look in the wrong places for God. We tend to wait for some loud, earthshattering way for God to speak, but God wants to speak in the soft, gentle breeze.

God gave Elijah a close friend. In verse 21 Elisha commits himself to the Lord's servant and the story concludes. He followed Elijah and ministered to him. Two prophets sharing the ministry together. As we can see, Elijah found his needed rest. He found companionship. He communicated with God.

Many of us started our Christian walk with confidence and faith. We were like the fellow whom Tim Hansel describes in <u>Eating Problems for Breakfast</u>. He was the sort of man who would go after Moby Dick with a row boat, a harpoon, and a jar of tartar sauce. However, it doesn't take long to start feeling discouraged for some of the very same reasons as Elijah. Are you facing the halfway mark in some task in your world? If you are halfway through paying off a debt, discouragement may catch you off guard as you lean on your shovel to rest. Are you overwhelmed by the task left before you? Whether you are knee-deep in crumbled bricks or desk-deep in memos and meetings, the debris of the daily routine can clutter your mind and keep you from seeing the work you have already accomplished. Have you lost your vision and your confidence? Are you feeling insecure about whether God is really going to help you when those problems attack you from all sides?

Discouragement has a strong, relentless power to pull the focus of our heart and minds in on ourselves. It can quench our hunger for knowing and trusting in Christ and lead us to trust in our own abilities. Don't let it. Follow Elijah's guidelines for encouragement and resume your task with renewed spirit.

CHAPTER NINE

MANAGING OUR MISTAKES

We Christians suffer from a very common ailment: making honest mistakes. I'm not talking now about willful sin. Mistakes can lead into sin, but honest mistakes are simply .... well, let's listen to Mr. Webster.

To make a mistake means "to choose wrongly," or "to make a wrong judgment." Webster amplifies this in a second meaning: "a wrong attitude, action, or statement proceeding from faulty judgment, inadequate knowledge or intention." Remember now, we're certainly not talking about out-and-out purposeful rebellion. We're certainly not talking about demonic deception. We're talking about honest-to-goodness, simple garden-variety mistakes--to which we are all prone. But these simple mistakes (as we shall see) frequently open the door to sinful activity. I have found five categories of mistakes illustrated in Scripture. Our mistakes, and some of the factors leading to those mistakes, are in these categories.

First   Panic-Prompted Mistakes

These are mistakes we invariably made out of fear, or from being in a hurry, or as a result of worry. We panic and make a wrong decision.

Look at Genesis 12:10. This mistake was made by Abraham. Remember that God had said to Abraham, "You are my man. Through you a nation will be born, and you will have a heritage like no other man that has lived, Abraham. Stand fast. Trust me through all the cares of life, and I will bring through your life a nation."

With that promise still ringing in his ears, Abraham panicked. We read: "Now there was a famine in the land." There was no bread and no meat. Apparently, there was not much water, either. Things had gotten tight. So Abraham made a mistake and went down to Egypt.

Why? He got shook. Even though God had said, "Abraham, you stay beside Me at the altar at Bethel, and I will make you a man of God, and through you I'll give birth to a nation," he panicked and headed south, for the famine was severe.

And when you make a "panic mistake," you simply make the first one, and it quickly leads to the next, like a row of dominoes. Enter the next!

And it came about when he came near to Egypt, that he said to Sarai his wife, "See now, I know that you are a beautiful woman; and it will come about when the Egyptians see you, that they will say, 'This is his wife'; and they will kill me, but they will let you live. Please say that you are my sister so that it may go well with me because of you, and that I may live on account of you" (Gen. 12:11-13).

Oh, we know that whether he will live or not doesn't depend on Sarah; he will live on account of God. But you see, when you move into Panic Palace, your whole focus gets twisted, and you forget what God has said. Instead, we give direct attention to what people say (rather than God) and what people think (rather than scripture).

Numbers 13 and 14 illustrate a second example of panic errors. The Hebrew spies went into the Promised Land to see if the children of Israel could take the country just beyond Kadesh Barnea, a border city. The spies came back with a U.S. Supreme Court sort of majority report. Ten said, "No way! There are giants in the land. Compared to them we're like little grasshoppers." Two of them said, "We can take that land. God gave it to us. It's a promised land!"

The people believed the majority report out of panic fear. They determined not to go into the land. And what happened? They were made to wander in the wilderness for forty years. They made a bad mistake; in this case it was out-and-out sin. But what prompted it was the mistake of listening to wrong counsel . . . and believing it.

I find that for us moderns, panic-prompted mistakes often have to do with two major issues: romance and finance.

Can't you hear the young woman saying, "I've come to that ripe old age of twenty-four and still haven't found a mate"? I know a number of people who are thirty-four and would be happy to trade off with her, because in panic they raced ahead of God and got themselves a mate. They wish they were back at age twenty-four now, unscarred and still available.

The matter of finances is an equally familiar problem. In panic we grab the first lifesaver loan we can get hold of. Before going down for the third time in a sea of debt, we just sort of bubble out, "Where are you, Lord? . . . ord? . . . d? . . . ?

If you are on one of those two precipices, sit tight. Stand fast. God knows what He is doing.

Second   "Good-Intentioned" Mistakes

Now, in a sense, all mistakes are like this if they are genuine mistakes. But let's categorize this one by itself: "good intentioned" mistakes. This is a mistake that is made ignorantly with an absolutely pure motive. You have good intentions, but you use the wrong planning or the wrong method.

Consider Moses, in Exodus 2. He's forty years old. (You never get to the place , even in the Bible, where you're too old to make mistakes!) Middle-aged Moses realizes he is potentially able to deliver God's people from the bondage of Egypt. So Moses rolls up his sleeves and, preempting Frank Sinatra by some 3,500 years, says, "I'll do it my way."

Now it came about in those days, when Moses had grown up, that he went out to his brethren and looked on their hard labors; and he saw an Egyptian beating a Hebrew, one of his brethren. So he looked this way and that, and when he saw there was no one around, he struck down the Egyptian and hid him in the sand (Ex. 2:11,12).

With the right motive (delivering the Hebrews, avenging the oppressed), he killed a man. After all, shouldn't he defend his Hebrew brother? His blood was Hebrew even though his whole culture was Egyptian. His desire was to defend what was right, but his good intentions led to tragedy: the sin of murder.

And you know what? Moses thought everybody would understand. That's another characteristic, by the way, of good intentioned mistakes. We have the feeling that "everybody will understand." But look at Acts 7. It's the same story about Moses but told 1,500 years later from a different vantage point:

But when he was approaching the age of forty, it entered his mind to visit his brethren, the sons of Israel. And when he saw one of them being treated unjustly, he defended him and took vengeance for the oppressed by striking down the Egyptian. And he supposed that his brethren understood that God was granting them deliverance through him: but they did not understand" (Acts 7:23-25, italics mine).

I'm not a prophet, but I've made enough mistakes in my life to be somewhat of an expert on the subject. With good intentions, you can plunge ahead and roll up your sleeves and do things in the flesh-and they will come back to haunt you. It's as if we decide to do God's will our way. Know what? That's not God's will!

I remember one time I was leading a Bible study group, somewhat like a seminar. We are sitting in a circle, and I suppose there were twenty people there. A couple of chairs were empty, and a fellow came to the door with a woman who appeared to be twenty years his senior. "You and your mother can sit right here," I said.

Wouldn't you know, it was his wife!

They left at the first coffee break. Friends and neighbors, I could have cut my tongue out. I had good intentions, but I didn't think.

Third   Negligent Mistakes

Men, we suffer from this one especially-passive, negligent mistakes. They occur in Scripture rather often, relating to the home, to the role of a father. Negligent mistakes are a results of laziness or oversight or inconsistency or just a plain lack of discipline.

Let me show you an illustration, and maybe you'll be shocked. (If I were just getting started in the Scripture, I would be shocked.) The man is David. In 1 Kings 1:5,6 we read:

Now Adonijah the son of Haggith exalted himself, [Haggith was David's wife-one of many, by the way. If you study the genealogy of David, you'll discover that this man was grossly guilty of polygamy. I count eighteen wives; there might well have been more. Some of those are not even named, but one of them was Haggith, the mother of Adonijah] saying, "I will be king." So he prepared for himself chariots and horsemen with fifty men to run before him.

And his father had never crossed him at any time by asking, "Why have you done so?"

Passive negligence.

Adonijah was born a rebel, grew up a rebel, and when he reached the "age of accountability" he refused to be accountable! He rebelled, saying, "I'll become king." Part of the problem was a father who never crossed the son. David never said to his son, "Son, you've got a bent toward rebellion. As your father, I am responsible before God to curb that bent, to deal with it until you yourself can get it under control."

No, David was like many dads. Too busy. Preoccupied. And therefore, negligent. It's a common mistake among successful, high-achieving fathers.

Benjamin Franklin once wrote these insightful words:

A little neglect may breed mischief: for want of a nail the shoe was lost; for want of a shoe the horse was lost; and for want of a horse the rider was lost.

That's the way negligence is.

Fourth   Unrestrained-Curiosity Mistakes

Of all the five categories of mistakes, this is probably the most attractive to young people, although it is not exclusively their problem. Unrestrained curiosity usually relates to the sensational or the demonic.

The whole world of curiosity is in on one sense a very creative part of our lives, but we are destined for trouble if curiosity is not restrained.

First Samuel 28 is the story of a king who had lost both his confidence and his power. When his friend Samuel died, King Saul sought to speak to Samuel through a spiritualist medium. He disguised himself and, taking two other men with him , he paid a visit to a woman seer by night. They purchased a contract with the netherworld, and before long they were in touch with the other world. It began as unrestrained curiosity-a costly mistake. It led to a horrible sin that ultimately became part of the cause of Saul's death (I Chron. 10:13, 14).

Fifth   Blind-Spot Mistakes

These are the ones we repeat most often, the ones we commit out of ignorance or habit or even poor parental influence. We're blinded to the truth and we stumble into this kind of thing time after time.

The last part of Acts 15 is the account of a conflict between two godly men, Paul and Barnabas. John Mark, Paul's earlier companion, had deserted him in the previous missionary journey. When they got ready to take the next missionary journey, the apostle Paul was discussing matters with Barnabas, who suggested they take John Mark with them. "No way!" said Paul.

In Paul's mind, John Mark was not profitable to him. Paul considered him a shipwreck, a fluke, a failure. He had a blind spot when it came to that weakness in other people. So he made a mistake. (Later in his ministry he was man enough to admit that Mark was profitable to him- 2 Tim. 4:11.)

There is perhaps an even clearer example of this kind of mistakes in Galatians 2:11-15. There's no need to go into any great depth of study; we just need to see the issue. Peter (called "Cephas" in the Galatians passage) had a blind spot when it came to the question of grace , especially as it related to his diet.

When he was around Jews, he ate good ole kosher cookin'. But when the Gentiles were there he'd stuff down the ham sandwiches and pigs feet like they were going out of style. He really couldn't let himself enjoy the full benefits of grace . . . but worse than that, he fell into a hypocritical life-style, doubtlessly justifying both the legalism and the liberty whenever necessary.

A mistake! Paul saw through it immediately and "opposed him to his face." Peter's response is not recorded, but one has little difficulty imagining his embarrassment. It is remarkable how "blind-spot" mistakes can be so obvious to everyone but the victim!

Of all the mistakes we make, this kind is the one we rationalize the most. We could probably pass a lie detector test because we are so convinced that we did the right thing.

A Psalm Of Balm-for the Mistaken

Psalm 31 was written, I believe, on a blue day in David's life. As we look at this psalm, we're going to see that he was broken and disappointed. He most likely wrote it on the heels of a mistake, maybe one he had made out of panic. Maybe it was one that was related to his home. Perhaps shortly after having a blind spot pointed out, he said:

In Thee, O Lord, I have taken refuge;

Let me never be ashamed; In Thy righteousness deliver me.

Incline Thine ear to me, rescue me quickly; Be Thou to me a rock of strength,

A stronghold to save me. For Thou art my rock and my fortress; For Thy name's sake Thou wilt lead me and guide me. . . .

Into Thy hand I commit my spirit (Ps. 31:1-3,5).

Familiar words? Sure, those last six were Jesus' very words as He was dying on Calvary. Just before he gave up his spirit, Jesus said to God, "To you I commit my spirit." It was the lowest point, physically and emotionally, in the entire life of the Messiah. But let's apply all this to our post-mistake depression periods in life.

You'll discover, after the grave and painful ramifications of making a mistakes, that it is only to God that you can commit your spirit at that time. No other person can give the comfort we need. On the heels of a mistake, get on your knees, fall before God, and lay out your shame and humiliation. No one else can heal you of that sense of shame and self-disappointment. The old songwriter was right: "No one understands like Jesus"-no one.

Now, from that perspective, let us observe how God views us when we've made those mistakes.

I hate those who regard vain idols; But I trust in the Lord.

I will rejoice and be glad in Thy lovingkindness,

Because Thou hast seen my affliction;

Thou hast known the troubles of my soul (Ps. 31:6,7).

First, God views us realistically. It is very helpful and important to remember that God sees us as we really are. We work so hard sometimes to keep the full truth from other people, for fear they will not understand. We burn up all kinds of emotional energy keeping our real selves from one another.

Mark Twain once wrote: "Everyone is a moon, and has a dark side which he never shows to anybody.: But God knows that dark side. God sees it plainly.

David said. "I rejoice, because you are realistic, Lord, when You see me. God know my bents. You know my tendencies. God know my sense of panic, my fears. God know how I was reared. God know the bad habits I have picked up. God know my track record. God you also know my intentions, not just my actions. God have seen my affliction."

The second thing I notice about God is that God views us thoroughly. "Thou hast seen my affliction; Thou hast known the troubles of my soul" (Ps. 31:7). I wonder if that was the place that old Negro spiritual got its start-" Nobody knows the trouble I seen, Nobody knows but Jesus. . . ."

God sees, afflictions have to do with the externals. Troubles have to do with the internals. "Lord, You see the whole world of affliction and God feels with me the trouble down inside." Remember that great statement regarding our Savior's understanding heart?

For we do not have a high priest who cannot sympathize with our weaknesses (Heb. 4:15).

There is great comfort in those words! But have you ever read two verses before that one? Verse 13 says that nothing is hidden from God's sight. Everything is laid bare to His eyes- and still He sympathizes with us! I'll tell you, that fills me with encouragement. Afflicted without and troubled within, mistake-prone though we are, He understands!

Seeing us realistically, seeing us thoroughly-how does God treat us?

Thou hast not given me over into the hand of the enemy (Ps. 31:8).

God does not reject us! That's the thing we fear the most, I believe, when we've made a mistake. If it's been a bad mistake, we especially fear divine rejection. We're afraid God is going to say, "That's it! Go to your room! Finished!" But David said:

Thou hast not given me over into the hand of the enemy; [and I love this part] Thou hast set my feet in a large place (Ps. 31:8).

That doesn't mean he had big feet. It means God gave him room. God doesn't crowd us. God gives us space.

Ever notice that when we try to find relief, people crowd us? They tighten the rope. They put very stringent limitations on us. They put a time limit on us or some other reminder of obligations. David said in this verse, "Lord You have a large place; You give me space; You give me room."

I want you to know that our heavenly Father is not anxious. God is quietly at ease and is calm while you are coming to your senses. God knows what God is doing. Isn't that a relief? It makes trusting God so much easier. No wonder David said:

> But as for me, I trust in Thee, O Lord (v. 14).

How does God instruct us when we make a mistake?

First, God instructs us in a context of trust, not suspicion. "I trust You, Lord." When you turn your situation over to people, there will often be suspicion that we will make the mistake again. People will be there with seventeen warnings, six sermons, two songs, and a poem to back them up-and a long, long index finger driving itself into your chest, saying, "You'd better watch that." God instructs us in a context of trust, not suspicion.

Second, God instructs us in all of life, not just the pleasant times. Are you ashamed, embarrassed, humiliated, failing, losing? Your times are in God's hands. God is instructing us in the bad times just as God does in the pleasant times. That's why James says, "Don't resent them [corrections] as intruders, but welcome them as friends" (James 1:2, Phillips).

Third, God instructs us in the secret places, not the public places.

> How great is Thy goodness,

> Which Thou hast stored up for those who fear Thee,

> Which Thou hast wrought for those who take refuge in Thee.

> Thou dost hide them in the secret place of Thy

presence from the conspiracies of people (Ps.31:19,20).

The best thing we learn from mistakes are learned in secret, for it is there God tell us God's secrets, and in doing so, covers us with God's love and understanding.

"Christians are not perfect, just forgiven" is one of the many bumper stickers we've seen. Frankly, I'm not too big on most of the stuff folks stick on their cars, but that one I like.

It came in handy recently. . . not on my car, but on the one weaving in and out of heavy freeway traffic last week. The guy was obviously late and irritated as he began to tailgate my car. I changed lanes so he could pass, and he darted into the space on my left.

At precisely the same time, another car shot into that same lane in front of him, and instead of plowing into that car, the speedy stranger pulled over in front of me-fast. I slammed on my brakes, almost got rear-ended, and barely missed his car-at fifty-five miles per hour!

Just then, he looked in his rear-view mirror and hunched down in his seat, embarrassed. I glanced at his bumper sticker and smiled down inside. It was perfect timing!

He backed off his breakneck pace, and I soon pulled up even with his car. I looked over at him and suddenly realized he was one of our church members (he had recognized me earlier in his mirror). I rolled down my windows, smiled, and yelled across the freeway- "You're forgiven, remember?" Relieved, he returned my smile.

Yes, not even becoming a Christian erases our imperfections. We still make mistakes-even dumb mistakes. But, thank God, forgiveness gives us hope. We still need a lot of it.

CHAPTER TEN

OVERCOMING THE DUNGEONS OF DEPRESSION

Charles Schultz has endeared himself to the American public with his humorous comic strip <u>Peanuts</u>. There was one that captured my mind, if you can recall, the very familiar booth in which Lucy has placed herself. It is wide with that familiar sign,"Psychiatrist Is In, 5 cents please," and Lucy sits behind it as Charlie Brown is in front, pouring out his trouble. I laughed because it reminded me of myself.

As you have noticed, we have been dealing with some interesting subjects as depression, temptation, worry, anger, and loneliness. Some of you may think there should be a sign that says, "Psychiatrist Is In, Free Advice." I do not want to give the impression that I am writing to give a quick fix or solve everyone's problem because some problems are complex and extremely involved. Some of you have suffered deeply from the problems discussed in this book, and by your reading this now, you have proven that this topic - and more importantly, what God has to say - is of interest to you. It may be true that in some cases we help one another very little, but in other cases God is using the Word in wonderful ways.

We are using the Word because we desire to learn of God's wisdom and hear what He has to say. If you need deep help, seek it because 30-45 minutes in reading is inadequate to deal with the deep-rooted pain some people have experienced.

My heart goes out to those in the Church who have suffered emotionally, physically, and/or spiritually, and we are have to thank the Lord that those of us who are healthy are here to endure this experience together. We will discuss the problem of depression through the lives of three men. We are interested in the life of Moses, Elijah, and Jonah. I pick these three men because ironically all three have suffered the same kind of depression. I have researched the writings of persons more qualified on the topic to define the problem. There are some to suffer with it and could do a better job of defining it, but others have never experienced much depression.

What is depression? I quote from a Christian clinical psychologist: "depression is undue sadness, dejection, melancholy feeling - a feeling of worthlessness, guilt, and apprehension. Depression is unrealistic grief - anxiety and unrealistic fear. Depression sometimes leads to suicide." Webster adds that "depression means feeling extreme discouragement, dejection, despair, and hopelessness." The feeling of depression which people, who have counsel with me, express is a feeling of hopelessness - all is loss, the desire to quit, give up - just can't make it in life.

These three men whom I am describing had these feelings. In Numbers 41, we consider the life of Moses and his experience with depression. Let's divide these persons into three parts. Each had a 1) physical reason; 2) emotional reason; and 3) spiritual reason. Thus, a spirit of hopelessness, grief, and depression.

For Moses, the people of Israel had been miraculously delivered from Egypt. They had been delivered though the Red Sea. They had been fed manna from heaven every morning; led by a cloud by day, and a fire by night. The entire experience could be summed up in the word, "miracle". They came now to this place where they despised manna. They griped about the food, water, path, sights around them, about the enemy, impossible future around them. If you can remember from your studies of Scripture they desired to return to Egypt where they longed for the leeks, garlic, onions - you have to be hungry to ask for these items.

Verse 10-15 gives the declaration that is unbelievable. "Lord, kill me!" I can't take it any longer. I quit, I resign. I'm finished." That's a depressed man. Why was he depressed and why did he want to die? Why did he feel so dejected and unwanted, willing to quit? First, there was a physical reason. Physically, Moses was exhausted. Moses never learned on his own the art of delegation. Moses tried to do all the work by himself. It is important for us to know our limitations and not try to do everything ourselves. Why did I say this about Moses? Because of what God says. In verse 16, God told Moses to gather seventy men who were elders amongst the people and to let them work with him. He was trying to do it all alone, so God told Moses to spread it out. He picked the men and very soon the burden was released. Delegation was an issue for Moses because earlier in his life, his father-in-law pointed out the same weakness in him - as revealed in Exodus 18:13. In the earlier part of this chapter, his father-in-law came to visit and it was a real blessing because he had the opportunity to observe Moses' actions. From morning until night, one after another, people were bringing their problems to Moses. In seeing this, the father-in-law asked "why are you doing this alone Moses? This is not good, for you will surely wear yourself out. You cannot handle it alone." Verse 19 has some excellent counsel in that you need to be the people's representative before God and teach the people to do things for themselves by following God's Word." Moses listened to this counsel and chose able men of all Israel and made them leaders over the people. Moses became wiser because of the visit from his father-in-law.

So, we see in Numbers 11 that Moses is exhausted, trying to do everything himself. Physically, he was tired. Emotionally, Moses had a problem - as seen in verse 15: "if you are going to deal thus with me, kill me at once and do not let me see my wretchedness." I suggest that Moses suffered from an inferiority complex at this time in his life. He said, "I can't do the job and I don't want to carry on the work. I ask you to kill me. I can't live like this." He felt very inadequate for the task.

J. Oswald Saunders in the excellent book "A Spiritual Clinic," makes a statement about Moses, which is worth repeating. So if you are suffering from depression, with inferiority feelings, this will hit you: "Moses overlooked the fact that God has made us responsible for our own perfection and not that of others." Have you ever been depressed because somebody else won't grow up? Here it is that you have a heart for God, and you pour your life into someone else, and they pass it off. You counsel with people and lay out what God says in His word, but they just walk away and ignored God's Word. This can be very depressing. Moses said, "Lord, I've worked with these people; I have poured my heart into them; and every time I turn around they are griping about the diet. They don't like the route we are taking. They don't like their leaders. They don't like the destination. They longed for what they had, and Moses felt drained and unequal to the task.

There was also a spiritual reason implied in verse 11. He felt distant from God. Spiritually, he felt that God was at a distance. Moses said to God, "why have You been so hard on me? or why have I not found favor in Your sight? God, what do you have against me? What did I do to deserve this? There are all kinds of disobedient people living around, but I try to obey you and I'm getting all the dirty ends of things. What's going on, Lord?" Moses felt that God was at a far distance, picking on him like a bully. If we go through enough difficulties on a constant basis and cannot find answers, we begin to feel picked on and that God has called our numbers. What is God's remedy to this problem? God's message to Moses is "let's spread out the work, and you back off and slow down. You are going so fast that you cannot find time to be with Me. Moses, relax, let seventy people do the work." Moses did exactly that, and the experience which followed was miraculous!! There is an old Greek motto that says, "You will break the bow if you keep it always bent". If our bow is always bent, we remain too close to the breaking point. When the Lord Jesus had the disciples come back from their teaching ministry, did He have a revival? no; another public ceremony? no; an autographing reception? no; a testimony period? no. Rather, what did He say? Christ said to the apostles, "let's come apart and rest." We should realize that if we don't come apart, then we will fall apart. Just as God told Moses, it is our responsibility to back off and delegate the work load when possible.

Now, let's look at Elijah who is one of my most favorite guys in Scripture. In chapter 19, we see what a great person Elijah was. He stood all alone; he stood up against a woman who ruled the land. King Ahab didn't rule the land as his wife, Jezebel, did. Elijah explained the famine which he had prophesied and had gone through a difficult time on Mount Carmel, where he had defiled the armies of Baal and had run down the mountain for solitude with God. Despite all of his labors, Elijah even became afraid and ended up in the desert. He was depressed and sad, "Lord, I quit! Take my life!" Physically, Elijah was exhausted - as was Moses. He had been facing the cult of Satan for quite a season. If you want something exhausting, try spending all day wrestling with the cults, and by the end of that day, you will sleep very well. All day long, he had been fighting the Baal worshipers. He had missed several meals, had made a thirty-mile run down to Jezreel. He had missed his sleep, missed his meals, had spent time in intense prayer, and had gone through a famine. Obviously, Elijah was exhausted. At the end of his role, I would like to suggest that he didn't suffer from an inferiority complex but rather from a martyr complex. He said in verse 4:10 that he felt alone, for there was no one else to take up the cause.

Have you ever made such a statement like this: everybody else is lazy, I'm the only one who is working. I'm the only one taking a stand at church, on the job, on my block!" That is exactly the Martyr's Complex, which implies "I am alone, for there is no one else to help me." That is a depressing thought. Spiritually, you will note that Elijah took his eyes off God and put them on his enemies. He had been criticized, and criticism will definitely depress you. First, Elijah felt that the whole world was against him, that God was against him, and that Jezebel was against him. Therefore, he concluded that "this was the end."

How does God handle it? God does not rebuke him. God is practical. The Lord fed him because he needed a good meal, and he was encouraged. The angel of the Lord provided for him and reminded him that he was not alone. The Lord told Elijah there are seven thousand I have not used yet.

Do you feel alone, as if in some niche which has people by the hundreds that are doing the job that we don't even know? We should not think that we are alone in any work. God also gave Elijah a friend. His name was Elisha. When we feel all alone and depression knocks at the door of our lives, when we are under the gun of depression and start to feel all alone, there is nothing like a friend who will minister unto us. Do you have a friend with whom you can share unconditionally? I dare say those who suffer deepest in depression have the fewest friends. The ministry of a friend is by someone who loves us, who doesn't preach to us, who rebukes us only in love, and loves to encourage and minister to us. God knew what Elijah needed, and He provided him with a friend.

Thus far we have learned that Moses had an inferiority complex, and Elijah had a martyr complex. Yet, there is another person from the Bible record, who is the most familiar among the minor prophets. In Jonah 4:1-11, Jonah had a superiority complex, which was his emotional hang-up. What we need to remember is that in each of the cases presented here, the men came off of a spiritual high. Moses came from Egypt and the Red Sea experience with clouds by day, fire by night, and manna from heaven - then he went into the slump of depression. Elijah came down from Mount Carmel, where the prophets of Baal had been silenced, and he went into a depression. Jonah came from his (the) greatest revival recorded in Scripture. The entire city of Nineveh had repented. (Most preachers would live on that for several months. I heard about the pastor who was voted the most humble pastor in America. The congregation gave him a medal that says, "To the Most Humble Pastor in America." Then they took it away from him on Sunday because he wore it.) Jonah could have been compared to this pastor, for he was the most successful evangelist in the world, but now he was in the slump of depression. We can't understand it.

Chapter 4 is a surprise passage because we probably expect Jonah to be thrilled but he was just the opposite. Understand clearly that physically, he was weary. He had walked across the city for three days, and must have been scorched from being in the belly of the fish. He preached the message of doom and people repented and that broke his heart. Jonah was displeased and became angry. Preaching can be an exhausting experience, and Elijah had done that for three days across the City of Nineveh, a heathen land known around the country. Verse 2 tells us why Jonah ran, for he never wanted Nineveh to repent, and he despised the heathen people. He was a prejudice nationalist, and it broke his heart when those people turned to God.   God did not bring judgment, but Jonah wanted God to take his life. To look at his situation, he was physically exhausted, emotionally bitter, and spiritually carnal - angry with God. If we live with bitterness and resentment, we will become just like Jonah. Spiritually, he was in a carnal state because he did not get his own way. Depression at times comes when we do not get our own way. We plan it this way and it happens that way - and that discourages us. If there is anyone in Scripture whom we would like to give a good shake, it is Jonah. But God did not do that. God was so gracious with Jonah. In verse 4, He asked Jonah, "do you have a good reason to be angry?" Jonah never answered God. He went and built a bed and was sitting under the hut in the city in which he had preached the revival. God appointed a plant to grow over the hut to deliver him from discomfort. He was so selfish that all he wanted was what he wanted. God then appointed a worm to attack the plant and it withered. The sun came up and beat down on Jonah's head, and he became faint and begged God again to die. "Death is better than life," to Jonah. God again asked him, "do you have a good reason to be angry about that plant?" God brought the fact before him and showed him that he had no reason at all to be angry.

Here are three men who went through tremendous depression, and all three asked to die. What lessons can we learn from them about depression? There are five lessons or ways to handle this issue when it arises.

1. Realize that depression is not a sin, it is a symptom. It would be similar to feeling as if a headache were a sin. Depression is not a sin, although your response to it can be. It is a symptom of something deeper. There is a root problem below that depression and God wants you to discover the root of it. Is it because you have been criticized? Is it because you feel all alone? Is it because you didn't get your own way? Is it because God did something that you didn't expect? Is it because you feel that God is picking on you? Is it because you are exhausted?

Some of the great people of God have suffered from depression. Listen to the words of Charles Spurgeon, "before any great achievement, a period of depression was very usual in my life. This was my experience when I became a pastor in London. My success appalled me. My great career cast me into the greatest depths of depression and caused me to utter misery, and I found no room for praise. This depression comes over me whenever the Lord is preparing a great blessing for my ministry."

Depression can be used to alert us that God has got something deeper for us. David was in a depression when he wrote some of his greatest Psalms. In the depressed state, you can find great comfort from the Psalms. Whenever you are depressed, ask God for insight into it.

2. Maintain a consistent program of relaxation and rest. This may involve some delegation. This may involve having fun and creating a sense of humor, not taking life so seriously. You may need to learn to relax more - stop flirting with depression if your life becomes your job and your job becomes your life. Those moments of physical exercise and relaxation profit quite a bit and we better take advantage of it.

3. Guard against these subtle complexities. Guard against feelings of inferiority; guard against feelings of martyrdom; and guard against feelings of superiority. We need to know that we are never alone, and then make an effort to develop a deep friendship with another Christian with whom you can share your life. Keep your eyes on the Lord, which will keep your eyes off the complexities of your own problem.

We can count on the fact that there will be times when our soul will be troubled. We will entertain thoughts that would surprise us: a) contemplating suicide - "God, take my life." b) at times, we are so troubled that our souls will not calm down. God can provide a companion who can calm the troubled waters of our souls. We gain perspective when we have somebody at our side. We gain objectivity, courage, and another opinion.

Thomas Coolridge says that "friendship is a sheltering tree. God did not accept Elijah's resignation. He gave him rest, good food, and a sheltering tree named Elisha, who ministered to him. Solomon says in Ecclesiastes 4:9-12, "two are better than one because together they can work more effectively. If one falls down, the other can help him up. But if one falls and is alone, no one can help him."

4. Remember that God is for us, not against us. Have you ever felt removed from God's awareness? It is like standing at the bottom of the Steinway looking up at total darkness. Even though one may call out, nothing happens. So often the one who is depressed feels totally unloved, useless, and rejected. Maybe we may feel as if God has abandoned us, and that all hope is gone. We may feel these things, but it doesn't mean our feelings are true.

So, how can we handle rough days when Satan tells us God does not care? I have found solid encouragement from Romans 8:31. "If God is for us, who can be against us." J.I. Packer - in his penetrating book, *Knowing God*, says this about this same Scripture, "the good news is that no opposition can crush us if God is for us. Who is God? God who is slow to anger, merciful, and abounding in steadfast love and faithfulness." Exodus 34:6 says, "I am God, and there is no other like Me. My council shall stand and I shall achieve all my purpose." God revealed His Sovereignty by bringing Abraham out of Ur; Israel out of captivity; and Jesus out of the grave. He is the one true God.

Let God fight for you. Satan likes to have Christians depressed and no longer effective for Christ.

5. Utilize the resources of the Word of God. Our adversary is relentless, determined and clever. He is also invincible. The same weapon Christ used to defeat Satan is available to us. That weapon is the Word of God. It is the only offensive weapon listed in Ephesians 6. The Word cuts and penetrates more than any other earthly weapon. You shall know the truth and the truth shall set you free. The strength found in the Word lies in the presence of God's Spirit; and the power of a good friend to be objective, provides companionship and encouragement and strength.

O, Jesus is a Rock in a weary land - a shelter in the time of storm.

CHAPTER ELEVEN

THE DENIAL OF DEATH

Death is a very fearful reality. I know of nothing more fearful, depressing, overwhelming, or discouraging than the reality of death in the mind of the person who is facing death. In this chapter I will be making reference to those who have a relationship with God versus those who do not recognize Jesus Christ, for God will deal with each one of us to remind us that ultimately we are going to die. Inevitably, we will pass into God's presence and face the future which is bleak if we do not know Jesus as Savior.

The very first communication God had with humanity had to do with death. The first time the Bible records a conversation which God had with Adam, He talked about death. God told Adam, "That every tree of the garden you can freely eat, but the tree of knowledge and evil you shall not eat, because the day do such, you will die." (Genesis 2:16-17)

At the very conclusion of the Bible, in the Revelation, God is still speaking about death. As He gives the picture of heaven, He says there will be no more tears, or sorrow or crying or death - those former things are passed away. The reason I mention it in this way is in the Bible from Genesis, the earliest part, to the Revelation, the last part - we have the subject of death woven through the fabric of God's Book. So when we talk about death and how we relate to it, we are not discussing something half way discussed in Scripture but something that is carefully developed. Let me lay a foundation in the first portion and then discuss what the Bible says about such matters as suicide, cremation, and the death of a child. Can the dead see us? What about baptism or praying to the dead? What about this matter of mercy killing? Let me first discuss four basic matters concerning death. In I Thessalonians 5:23, it gives the definition of death. What do we mean and what does God mean by death? Let's see how God has made us as human beings.

In verse 23, Paul says, "May our spirit, soul and body be preserved completely." Without getting into the intricate details between body and soul, which is almost as important as how many angels can dance on the head of a pin, it is important that we notice how God has made us in two parts. A part of us is invisible, inward, and intangible, and it is called here the soul and the spirit, so let's call this portion the soul/spirit. God has given every one of us a soul/spirit. A life principle that is eternal which we receive at the time of conception and we have it forever. This invisible part of us makes us what we are in our personality, in our inward being. Then God has made us with a body which could be called the anatomy, the tangible, the outward part. So, we have an inward part which cannot be seen except by God and that determines who we really are. Then we have an outer shell that is made up of skin and muscles, blood, bones - a body which is seen by man. Paul talks about all these right here. In Hebrews 4:12 he suggests the impact of the Word of God, the Bible. It tells us that God's Word is alive, active, and doing a work. The work which the Bible does pierces in the very being of humanity like a sword with two edges. It is able to penetrate what the scalpel of the surgeon can never penetrate; it is able to get into the inward part of us and do a job - of conviction, rebuke, blessing or change. God's Word is able to drive to the very heart of a matter in the area of our conscience, which cannot be done on any operating table - for only God can operate on the human conscience.

Inside of us is that inward being called the soul/spirit, and we also have an outward part called the joint marrow. For example, a glove fitted on my hand is not my hand although it may look like my hand. It is the wrapping that goes around what is my real hand. Let's look at the question, when does death take place? When the soul/spirit - the real me - leaves the shell, the wrapping called the body. This is so important to understand because of the way we have funerals and the way we look at death. It is important that we do not forget this illustration because it is crucial to our understanding of death. When the soul/spirit leaves the body, death has taken place - but as long as the soul/spirit rests within the shell, there is life. When death actually occurs, the soul/spirit leaves and goes to the life beyond, just the body remains. The body waits for the change, for the time known as the resurrection. It is the body that is placed in the casket - which like the glove is the shell, the tent, the wrapping - and we place it in a casket, put in the grave, and cover it with dirt. That is not really the person, for the real person is already in the presence of his/her destiny. So you see, when death occurs there is a separation which takes place.

Throughout the Bible, the idea of death and separation are used interchangeably. When we have death, we have separation. This is more adequately illustrated by Christ on the cross. It was the thief who said to Jesus, "Remember me when you come into your kingdom." Jesus looked at him and said, "This day, you will be with me in Paradise." That was a promise, not a statement. How could this be if His body remained on the Cross, but the real person went with God into destiny. That is why Jesus said at the end of His life, "Father, into thy hand I commend my Spirit." Surely He breathed His last breath and his soul departed. His body remained bound and wrapped in cloth and placed in a tomb. That was not the Lord Jesus because the real being was in another place. So you see, death is when the soul/spirit separates from the body.

How extensive is death? Is it going to affect everyone? Romans 5 is the classic statement in all Scripture in answer to this question. Does everyone die? Verse 12 says that death through sin spreads to all persons. Death and sin are Siamese twins, always going together. The first person mentioned is Adam through whom sin entered the world. When Adam sinned in the Garden the result was sin death. God told Adam, "you will surely die." He instantly died spiritually and began to die physically. I am convinced that if there were no sins there would be no death. Adam's sin spread to all persons and therefore death also spread to all persons.

I Corinthians 15:21-22 gives us the rule that all die, and what will be left of us is a glove, the shell or the body, but the real us will go on. But just as it happens, in each rule there are exceptions. Remember, there were several persons in the Old Testament who never died. Enoch and Elisha missed death. They bypassed the grave and went directly in the Lord's presence. Some of us who are alive might do the same according to I Corinthians 15:50. The body as we know it today cannot inherit eternal life. The old, perishable body cannot inherit an imperishable eternity. There must be a change, therefore there is a mystery - Awe will not all die but we shall all be changed." Our bodies will undergo a radical change in order to endure eternity. When will this happen? It will happen when Christ comes in the clouds for God's children, commonly called, the Rapture of the Church. The next event of the future will be that time when Christ comes in the clouds and carries off the earth all those who are believers and all those who have died in the Lord.

There will be a family reunion in the air, and we will be joined by those whom we love and those we never knew, to be forever with the Lord. What a tremendous hope! The only way to prepare for the separation of hand from the glove - soul/spirit from the body - is to accept the love of Christ. Nothing can be changed after death. Just a minute: do we realize it will happen one of these days? There will be a traffic disaster on the freeway. Talk about chaos. It will be interesting to see how many come to church the following Sunday. The mask will be ripped off at the rapture because God will only judge the heart not the outward appearance. The basic of going into the Lord's presence is believing in Christ as the ticket. What then shall be the result?

In II Corinthians 5, here the distinction must be made that what happens after death is dependent upon what happened before death between God and God's people. If we do not know the Lord personally, our destiny is all together different from the person who knows the Lord. Let me speak first of those who know Jesus Christ. This passage teaches that the Lord will prepare for us a certain kind of shell or wrapping that will be able to make it through time. No face lifting needed, no wrinkles. We all have groans, whether it is through headaches or heartaches - the fact is we all hurt. We should long to be clothed with our dwelling from heaven where there will be no hurt, no groans, no more nakedness.

Verse 6 answers what happens when we die? As long as we are at home in the glove, we are absent from the Lord. But if we absence ourselves from the body, we are present with the Lord. The next time we lay to rest a loved one, that person who knows Jesus as Lord, is with the Lord. There is no wait; there is no period of time for that person to earn his/her way or become prayed into. The person is instantly in the presence of the Lord. As Jesus said to that thief, "This day you will be with Me in paradise."

Psalm 116:15 is the best commentary on the death of a saint. "Precious in the sight of God is the death of His saints." Even if we die knowing there are heartaches and pain in our lives, God says we are highly to be prized. Revelation 20:11-15 states for us the ultimate end of the person who doesn't know the Lord. When we do not know the Lord and we pass away, we pass into a place in Scripture called Torment. A place of conscious, awesome terrible existence and we remain in our soul/spirit in that place until the ultimate doom is pronounced. One of the most mistaken ideas people have today is that only the Christian has eternal life. On the contrary, every one of us has eternal life; however, the lost person has eternal life in the lake of fire - whereas, the Christian has eternal life in the presence of the Lord.

The question often asked is how can a God of love enjoy tormenting people forever? First of all, the question is always off base, for the Bible never states that God takes pleasure in people's suffering. Secondly, the Bible did not state that God personally torments people. It is the loneliness, the aches, the abandonment, and the awful memories that plague each person throughout eternity. God does not stand over hell and laugh with glee over the destiny of the lost person. As a matter of fact, the flip side is that God is also a God of justice and of holiness. God has set down His plan, and if one refuses to abide by it, one must be willing to bear the consequences.

What then about funerals and memorials? I think these ideas need a face lift. We need to rethink this matter of funerals completely. We need to get away from the pagan things that frequently dictate the purpose of our funeral services. First of all, we should realize that we are dealing with the shell, not the person. Philippians 1:20 suggests the possibility of planning our death or at least our funeral. It would be beneficial to write down some ideas concerning arrangements and discuss with the family so that it is understood. This verse gives the basis to make the following comments. I want Christ to be exalted in my death. I want my body to exalt Christ when I am gone. How can it best do that? First, regarding the body, what profit is an open casket? As a pastor, when there is an open casket there are frequently deep personal, emotional attachments connected with the body. I have seen unbelievable things done at funerals. Parents have forced children to kiss the remains. I have seen mothers reach in and try to pull the body out of the casket; fainting that would have never taken place if the casket was sealed shut. Why is there viewing of the shell, since death is not really the body and since the person's spirit is with the Lord? Why exalt the shell in any way? Why have that as the final memory of the person? When God buried Moses, He did it in secret whereby, no one could find the body. The people remembered Moses for who and what he was in life. I suggest a time for a private grave side service for the family not to be revisited because that will be changed, as it actually becomes resurrection ground for God's power. I then suggest having a service without a casket or with a sealed casket. A service of praise and testimonies saying what the loved one's life meant to different ones who were ministered to by the person.

One other thought is that so much money is poured into funerals and it would be better to keep it simple. The family should take the money that is to buy the array of flowers, which will be wilted in a few hours, and give it to something that will live on. How about putting a statement of our faith in the will? How about sending out with the announcement of the loved one's death a clear presentation of that persons testimony for Christ. When the will is read people will hear more than what they expected. We should establish in our will the idea where we stand spiritually.

Paul says when the believer dies, we are not to grieve as those who have no hope. But how often Christian homes are filled with grief. A maverick idea would be at the service to have pictures of the persons life showing what he/she has done for Christ. We should be distinct, refusing to fall in that reckless tide. Fox's Book of Martyrs is filled with the name of persons who paid the ultimate price in their lives and have passed into the Lord's presence. So, whether in life or in death we should do all in such a way that God gets the glory. This should be the Christian epithet; however, the epithet of the lost person would read like the one I saw recently, which says "You cannot win." Obviously, that person did not hear the good news that we can win. Death is not the last thing, it is the gateway into everything. Let me use the remainder of this chapter to answer some of the commonly asked questions about death.

What about Suicide?

What can we say concerning the destruction of one's self. Let me quote Carl Barth when he says in his book <u>Church Dogmatics,</u> "to deprive a person of his/her life is a matter for the one who gave it and not the person themselves." We must start with the unequivocal fact that when self-destruction is the exercise of a supposed sovereignty of persons over themselves, it is an arbitrary criminal violation of the commandment and therefore self-murder." When we take the right upon ourselves to destroy ourselves, we have violated in criminal fashion the right that is not ours. It is God's right to take life, as it is His perogative to give life.

Dietrich Bonhoeffer in his work <u>Ethics</u> says, "A person who is on the brink of suicide no longer has an ear for commands or probation." A person who is desperate cannot be saved by laws that appeal to his/her own strength. One who despairs of life can be helped by the offer of a new life, which is to be lived not by one's own strength but by the grace of God." What he is saying is that we cannot legislate people out of suicide. When a person is at the brink of suicide that person needs help, attention, love, and the promise of grace - not more law or commands - but assistance.

Suicide is the most cowardly act performed against our loved ones, and it leaves a damaged stigma against Christianity - if the person is a Christian - because the devil takes this information to explode it and exploit it to the farthest extreme. So, as a Christian, when suicidal thoughts come we must remember they are not of God. God is not the author of murder and self destruction, for they are of the devil. Help must be sought, whether it be professionally or from God's Word, a pastor, or close friends. But do not tolerate these feelings because they do not get easier, as a matter of fact they get harder.

Remember no one lives to himself/herself and no one dies to himself/herself. We cannot die by taking our own lives without leaving a tragic wake in the experience of our closest loved ones. More and more, our lives and our children's lives are being touched by this kind of death along with the questions that ripple from it. Questions like what kind of people commit suicide? Why do they do it? Is this the unpardonable sin? Let's attempt to use God's Word to find some answers.

The Scriptures record several cases of people who took their own lives. For example, Saul (I Samuel 31:4); Ahithophel (II Samuel 17:23); and Judas Iscariot (Matthew 27:3-5). From these examples we can glean some important observations that, first of all, believers as well as non-believers commit suicide. Secondly, excruciating circumstances often surround the person who commits suicide. Thirdly, in the cases of Saul and Judas, there was probably some kind of satanic or demonic influence. Since Satan is both a murderer and a liar, and since Saul and Judas have been involved with Satan, it stands to reason that they had been deluded into destroying themselves by the father of lies.

Of course, there are many other reasons why a person might choose to commit suicide: feelings of utter hopelessness, loneliness, depression, revenge or possibly even manipulation. But regardless of the reasons, to take away a person's life is up to the one who gave that life (Psalm 139:16).

What about the Death of Young Children?

What happens to the baby who lives only a few hours, or a few months? What is the destiny of the child who dies before being able to discern right from wrong, before reaching the age of accountability? Let's take a look at the only case in the Bible that deals specifically with the destiny of an infant.

II Samuel 12 is the account of God's judgment upon David for his adultery with Bathsheba. One of the heartbreaking consequences of David's sin was that the child of that union would die. Nevertheless, from the time the child grew ill until death seven days later, David fasted and wept, asking God to spare the baby's life. Once the terrible week was over, however, David resumed his meals and his life. David clearly identified the destiny of this child when he says, I shall go to him." The child was already in the presence of the Lord where David knew he himself would go when he died.

In Matthew 19:13-14 children were brought to Jesus and the disciples refused them. For this act Jesus rebuked them saying, "Suffer the children and forbid them not to come unto me because unto such belong the kingdom of God." This verse is clearly a promise. That the kingdom of heaven is the property of ones such as these little children. It is clear that when a child dies, the individual skips into God's presence.

What About Cremation?

What is cremation? It is the act of burning and reducing to ashes the body of one who has died. The process is known to many. There is a specially made vessel in which the body is placed and put into a furnace that is heated to 2000-2500 degrees - so that the entire body is reduced to a small heap of ashes. The ashes are then placed in an urn and enclosed by the family in a well-kept building.

What does the Scripture say about cremation? I say, nothing directly. I don't know of a case in Scripture where there was anyone cremated. Although, there were several occasions when persons were burned to death alive, but that is not the same practice. This practice is called "passing through fire" and it was part of an idolatrous, pagan act (II Kings 16:2-3). There is also another reason in Scripture for some people being burned, and it, too, is connected with disobedience. In these cases, God brings fire on individuals in judgment, Numbers 11:1 and Genesis 19:24. Neither of these is cremation, but it is interesting to note that the association of fire with the body seems to be connected with disobedience (John 7:15-26).

Burial seems to be the predominant method of caring for the dead throughout the Bible. For example, Abraham buried Sarah, and Jacob buried Rebekah; and even when Moses died, God used the method of burial to take care of his body. There were also two burials found in the New Testament - that of Lazarus and the Lord Jesus.

How did cremation get started if the biblical method seems to be that of burial? Anglo-Saxons received their concepts of cremation from the Vikings. The ones who died were placed on that ship which was tattered and beaten from the battle. The ship was then pushed out to sea and burned until it sank into the sea. However, the oldest method of cremation was recorded in India, where it went on for centuries. They claim it was because of sanitary reasons, the lack of cemetery space, and to curtail the spread of diseases.

So we see, there are two sides to this matter, yet nothing specifically stated in Scripture indicating that cremation is wrong.

There is one more thought to be considered. There seems to be the association of disobedience with the burning of a body. In America, cremation was made possible by those who openly denied the power of God in resurrection. It was an act of open defiance by the rationalist, the atheist, or the humanist that became a part of our country in the early seventeenth century. This defiance act conveyed the belief that this act would hinder God from raising the dead.

In summary, there is nothing in Scripture which says it is sinful. However, the association makes it questionable. It would be highly irregular for a believer to want to be cremated based on the multiplicity of references in the Bible relating to burial, not cremation. It is important to note that God is not limited to a body being buried before God can raise it up. A body can be blown into one thousand pieces in a bombing, but when the Day of Resurrection comes, the Lord will make that body from nothing. He has no difficulty in putting it back together from what we would call nothing.

What About Soul Sleep?

The concept of soul sleep was made popular by the Seventh Day Adventist and Jehovah's Witness. It is the belief that a person's soul is dormant, or asleep, from the time the body dies until the time of resurrection. This is believed by many today that the soul/spirit is not active, and when the body dies, it falls asleep and it remains that way during the time the body is in the grave, until the resurrection.

What Scriptures would be used to verify this belief? There are several. All those Scriptures refer to death as "sleep." For example, there is Job 14:12; Daniel 12:2; and I Thessalonians 4:13. These passages imply that when the body dies the soul sleeps. In John 11:1, I believe the soul/spirit never sleeps but it is continuously active and awake. This is the story of the death and raising of Lazarus, and Jesus is talking about the death of his friend. Since He uses the word sleep here there is a misinterpretation. Those around took the term literally. Remember that Lazarus, upon Jesus' arrival, was in the grave for four days. If Jesus had meant that Lazarus' soul was asleep, it would have made no sense for Martha to indicate there was a stench. It was the body that was asleep. In every case in Scripture where sleep is used referring to the dead, it is speaking about the body, not to the soul.

Another passage would be Luke 16:19-31 where Jesus tells the story of the rich man Lazarus, where the angels carried the soul to the bosom of Abraham. The verse following says the rich man died and went to Hades. He lifted up his eyes, being in torment. If his soul were asleep he would not be in torment. This even makes sense in our daily lives when we go to sleep at night. Our spirits won't sleep. Physicians and psychologists tell us where the dreams come from. They tell us that we dream every night, and if the soul/spirit was asleep, dreaming would not take place. The body rests and it must be dormant for a time during each 24-hour period, but the soul/spirit is always awake. Therefore, let it be understood that according to the Scripture, the soul/spirit - as soon as we pass from this earth - it is instantly absent from the body. Christians go to be with the Lord, while non-believers find their ultimate destiny in Hades, awaiting the final judgment at the Resurrection.

What About Reincarnation?

Reincarnation is becoming very popular today. It is amazing how many great individuals believe in such a thing as this. Reincarnation teaches that the soul/spirit returns from beyond to re-inhabit another body or another form. How does a person believe this and yet believe in the Bible? Well, the Bible tells us in John 3 that Jesus taught Nicodemus to be born again. If we believe it, this is one of the proof texts in which a person who wants to embrace Scripture and reincarnation that person will go to John 3 and say even Jesus taught a person must be born again - especially by the Spirit. The conclusion here is the belief that the Spirit can re-enter a person's life. Hindu teaches that one spirit may be reincarnated as many as six hundred thousand times. That seems as if it would wear out a spirit to return so many times, once is enough!

What can we say about reincarnation? The Bible says there is only one earthly existence. Romans 6:23 and Hebrews 9:27 both state that we live and die once, so there seems to be finality to this life. But I just danced with glee when I found Job 7:8-10. "The eye of him who sees Me will behold Me no more. Thine eyes will behold Me but will see Me no more." When a cloud vanishes it is gone, so he who goes down to Sheol does not come up. He will not return again to his house, nor will his place know him anymore. We know from the context of this book that Job believed in a future resurrection. Therefore, it is obvious that he is referring here to the fact that a person dies once and does not come back in this world. What is our answer to those who think they have adequate proof that people relive in different form? My only answer is demonism. Demons are timeless and ageless.

Demonic activity that was involved in the 16th century could reform and re-enter our bodies in the 17th and 20th century.

What About the Prayers for the Death and Baptism of the Dead?

First, prayers for the dead refer to offering prayers on behalf of those who have passed on in hopes of making their destiny brighter. This is a teaching of the Roman Church. It never finds it basis in Scripture. There is never a time when someone prayed for the dead in Scripture or hoped to relieve someone gone from this earth by prayer. Then how could a church teach that there are prayers for the dead? The Roman Church find their basis for prayer for the dead in a book called Second Maccabees. It is one of the Non-Canonical books in the set of the Apocrypha, written between the Old and New Testaments. At the end of the writing of Maccabees and before Matthew, there are 400 years that passed. There were many books written by Jewish historians, poets and others and these books have been embraced by the Roman Church as being inspired Canonical books. One of the books is entitled Second Maccabees, which tells the story of a group of soldiers who were wounded in battle and died. Then there were these Jewish friends who prayed for them, so as to assist them in finding a better life after death. This is where purgatory got its name. The belief that in such place, the soul is purified and ultimately finds a blissful existence rather than a miserable one. Through the process of masses and other religious rites, a person's destiny after death can be altered. We would not accept it because we do not believe that the Apocrypha is inspired by God and is not quoted as inspired Scripture throughout the New Testament.

But this matter of baptism for the dead, however, is interesting because it is a scriptural statement. Look at I Corinthians 15:29, "Otherwise what will those do who are baptized for the dead?" If the dead are not raised at all why then, is there baptism for them? This chapter is the greatest in the Bible on the Resurrection of the body. Those in the days of Paul were under tremendous persecution and often experienced martyrdom right after they came to know Christ and before they could be baptized. It is because of such a concern for those at Corinth that they personally, as a representative of those who have been martyred, would be baptized on their behalf. It is interesting that Paul does not condone this. He simply stated it as something they were doing and saying to them in this chapter about the resurrection. If there is no resurrection for the dead, why are you baptizing yourselves on behalf of those who already died? If you are saying there is no resurrection, why engage yourself in this representative baptism?

Paul does not say he approved of this practice. He sees it only as proof that those people firmly believed in the resurrection. He is using this verse as an agreement in favor of the resurrection. He says that we believe it and if we didn't believe it, you would not be representing someone that passed on, being their representative in baptism.

In answering these questions, I am not concerned with whether you agree with me or not, or whether we have these questions answered in their totality. My concern is whether we are ready for the inevitable that is before us! Death is real and as certain as the breath in our lungs. If Christ does not return, death is coming. Death transforms all values, and instantly changes everything around us. The question we each need to answer is "am I ready to die?" If your answer is "I am ready," then ask "are my values straight?" In death, worthless things become priceless and priceless things become worthless. Only Christ can adequately prepare us for death. If any of us are not ready, this would be the perfect time to accept Christ and become prepared.

Wisdom	Temptation	Bitterness
Ps. 25:4-5a	Prov. 16:32;25:28	"unforgiveness forms
Ps. 119:130, 135	I Cor. 10:13	a root of bitterness"
Prov. 1:23; 2:6,7	Heb. 2:18	Isa. 55:7
Prov. 6:23	Heb. 4:16	Mt. 6:14, 15
Prov. 9:10	Jas. 1:2-3	Mt. 18:35
Jn. 14:26	Jas. 1:12-14	Mk. 11:25, 26
I Cor. 2:16b	II Pet. 2:9	Jn. 20:23
Eph. 1:17		
Jas. 3:17		
I Jn. 2:27		

Worry	Inferiority	Discouragement
Ps. 29:11	Ps. 107:9	Deut. 31:6, 8
Ps. 55:18	Prov. 12:25	Ps. 107:19
Prov. 3:1,2	Mt. 6:34	Isa.41:10,13
Isa. 26:3,12	Mt. 28:20	Mt. 6:33
Isa. 32:17,18	Lk. 12:31	Mt. 11:28
Isa. 57:21	Phil. 4:6,7	I Cor. 2:9
I Cor. 7:15	Eph. 3:11,12	Phil. 1:6
Eph. 2:14	I Pet. 5:7	Phil. 4:6
Phil 4:7		Heb. 13:5
II Tbes. 3:16		I Jn. 5:4

Managing Mistakes	Depression	Death
Prov. 1: 2,5	Ps. 9:9,10	Ps. 23:4,6
Prov. 2:2,7	Ps. 146:8	Ps. 116:15
Prov. 3:16	Ps. 31:24	Prov. 14:32
Prov. 4:6,8,9	Is. 26:3	Jn. 5:21, 24, 25
Prov. 4:11-13	Is. 35:3,4	Jn. 5:28
Prov. 4:25,26	Is. 50:10	Jn. 11:25, 26
I Cor. 1:30	Is. 60:1	I Cor. 15:53, 54
Eph. 5:15, 16	Jer. 29:11, 13	I Cor. 15: 56, 57
Ja. 1:5, 6, 9	Lk. 4:18, 19	II Cor. 5:8
	Jn. 14:27	Heb. 2:14, 15
	Phil. 2:5	Heb. 9:27
	Eph. 4:23, 24	Phil. 1:21

To contact Dr. Clive E. Neil for speaking engagements, seminars or to receive other books and teaching tape series of his, please call:

Bedford Central Presbyterian Church

1200 Dean Street & Nostrand

Brooklyn, New York 11216

(718) 467-0740

(718) 467-3651